Sonder

A Novel

SONDER

A Novel

By Jes Pan

Paperclip Publishing LLC
Chandler, AZ

Sonder

Copyright © 2022 by Jes Pan

Published by: Paperclip Publishing LLC

Editor: Noelle S. LeBlanc
Cover Design: Keenan S. Peebles
Interior Typography: Hannah Thigpen

Library of Congress Control Number: 2022940729

ISBN: 979-8-88589-192-9 (paperback)
ISBN: 979-8-88589-191-2 (hardcover)
ISBN: 979-8-88589-180-6 (eBook)

Printed in Rephen Printing, Co. LTD in Guangzhou and the United States of America

First Printing: 2022

Paperclip Publishing LLC
3800 W Ray Road Suite 5
Chandler, AZ 85226

www.paperclippublishing.com

To my grandma, Ami, for supporting every single one of my creative endeavors since I was born. I think you may have known I could do this before I did. Thanks for reading my book even though horror grosses you out. I love you more than applesauce.

To my wife, Sydney, for letting me shove chapters under your nose as soon as you come home from work, and always listening—really LISTENING—to my weird ramblings that might turn into books some day. Thank you for always being my soft place to land. You're my favorite, and I love you so very, very many.

DISCLAIMER:

This book contains graphic material related to extreme horror, gore, violence, and animal abuse, and may not be suitable for some readers. Reader discretion is advised.

CONTENTS

PROLOGUE

Allegra

September 1995

I remember this day because I was wearing a new shirt from the mall. It had a design of sequin flowers all over it. I had also just gotten my first grown-up haircut at the salon my mom liked, not the place where you sit in a plastic airplane. I remember this day because at six years old, it was the first time that my appearance had made me feel confident.

My dad worked overnight, from closing time until just before opening, in a bakery. He cleaned the counters, swept the floors, and most importantly, prepared the pastry dough for the following day. He liked to take me to school when he got home from work, then pick me up after he'd slept and showered. I liked it too because he always smelled like frying oil and powdered sugar in the mornings. More often than not, I would find a small white bag of doughnut holes on my seat in the car.

On this day, the one I remember because of the new shirt and the haircut, Dad brought me home from kindergarten and we found Mom having some kind of manic episode in the living room. She wasn't usually manic. My mom was the kind of person who would rather have a three-hour-long, measured and calculated conversation than a fight that could be over in fifteen minutes. But there she was, tripping over furniture with a towel in one hand and a fly swatter in the other. Her bronze curls flew out from her head at dozens of odd angles. As soon as Dad and I walked in she breathlessly explained, "Horsefly…in here. Trying to get it!"

Something on our side of the room caught her eye and she dashed between Dad and me. When she moved, I noticed a broken vase on the floor behind her, artificial orange flowers strewn across the wood floor. How long had she been at this?

Dad just sort of chuckled and climbed the stairs to their bedroom. His demeanor gave me the feeling he had seen her like this before. He seemed unconcerned, almost entertained.

Mom leapt at the front window and smacked it with the fly swatter. She checked the swatter and sighed with frustration when she saw it was clean. She surveyed the room, trying to find the enemy's new resting place. After a moment, she zeroed in on me.

"Allegra," she said, inching toward me. "Don't move."

The way she stared at me was so intense and severe. If I had a picture of that stare, I would never look at it. She held her gaze on me for several seconds before tearing her eyes away and looking toward the doorway that separated the living room from the kitchen.

"Shit," she whispered, taking a few steps in that direction. She looked back at my stunned expression, lowered her arms, and explained. "It was on your hair clip. Oh, honey, did you think I was about to smack you with this?"

Oh… She hadn't been looking at me that way at all. It was the fly. I guessed I believed that it had landed on my barrette, but I hadn't heard any buzzing.

"Sorry, Ally," Mom said as she walked into the kitchen. "I just can't handle an insect in my house. Makes the whole place seem…disgusting."

Before she disappeared around the corner, Mom lashed out with a particularly hard strike of the fly swatter. It thwacked against the wall, and she groaned in defeat. As I settled onto the couch with my rainbow zebra homework planner, I considered the possibility that some pests are simply impossible to catch.

PART ONE

CHAPTER 1

Allegra

March 2007

"Ally, I think I'm in love with you," Alex told me.

"Okay." I nodded, rustling the pillows.

"What, that's it?" He snaked his arms around my bare torso and pulled me closer. "I tell you I think I'm in love with you, and you just say *okay*?"

"Well, yeah. I mean, I think a lot of things. When we were doing it just now, I *thought* it might be fun to go out for apple pie afterward. Unless you want to do it again, that is."

Alex's face changed from hopeful to dejected the same way every guy's face changes when you don't declare that you love them too. I wanted to ask how rejection felt. I recognized it all over his face, caused by the lack of four tiny words from me, but how did it *feel*? Did it hurt? I mean, I knew from movies and books that it hurt, but *how* did it hurt? In what way?

"Come on, don't pout." I kissed him hard on the mouth.

Alex was a good-looking guy. Muscular without too many sharp angles. His features were symmetrical for the most part. His teeth were white and straight, eyebrows not too bushy, nose not too pointed. His eyes were a light, clear shade of blue, and natural highlights from his time spent outside on the lacrosse field softened the look of his brown hair. He was nice, too. Polite. Smart. An interesting conversationalist. But, did I love him? Absolutely fucking not. I didn't even really know why I had sex with him once a week, but it happened every Friday afternoon like clockwork.

Alex took my kissing him as a clue that I was still in the mood, and I wasn't *not* turned on by his enthusiasm, so I let him go down on me. He was surprisingly good at it for a high school boy. He made me come hard enough that I thought about saying nothing, but I couldn't let this go on. Not now that he'd involved the L word.

He crawled back up and laid his head on the pillow next to mine. I settled against him and counted to forty-eight in my head, slowly. Then I said, "I don't think we should see each other anymore."

The only downside to breaking up with Alex was having to take the bus home wearing nothing but my dance team leotard and a short denim skirt. I had black cotton pants in my bag, but they were still damp with sweat from practice and I didn't want to be damp on the bus.

A balding man in a necktie stood a little too close to me at the bus stop. I wondered if he could smell the pheromones on me. Normal girls get freaked out when men do things like this, but I'd always found it entertaining. As far as I was concerned, men like this could play out whatever fantasy they pleased about me inside their head. They knew they could never get a girl like me in real life. Necktie probably went home to a fat wife and ugly, untalented kids with lisps. *Who knows*, I thought as he 'accidentally' brushed my chest while stepping onto the bus, *maybe some time I'll give one of these guys a thrill and sleep with them.* But for today, I just flipped my blonde hair over my shoulder and claimed a window seat far away from Necktie. He was still watching me.

I rode the bus for twenty stupid minutes and then walked for another ten before reaching my front door. I was pissed because I had to ride the bus and annoyed at Alex for not still offering to drive me home, but at least I was being exposed to sunlight and maintaining my tan. I let myself in the front door with the key Mom had given me when I was ten. The personalization, pink paint and rhinestones, had held up surprisingly well for seven years.

"Hey, it's me!" I bellowed into the empty house. I knew no one was there, but I wanted to hear my voice echo back to me. I'd been coming home to an empty house for years. I liked it that way; more time to myself.

The first stop was my room. I kicked off my thin flip-flops and dropped my backpack on the floor. There was nothing hanging on my white walls, no knick-knacks on the desk, no suspicious titles on the bookshelf. My room was so plain that I'd even overheard my parents discussing whether it was normal for a young girl not to want to decorate. That had been several years ago, and probably not of real concern to them since they never even brought it up to me. Anyway, I was about to graduate high school, and soon after that, I would turn eighteen. However I chose to adorn my walls was officially my own damn business.

I wandered into my little brother's room next. Toby was probably at one of his nerdy little friends' houses discussing how Eli Roth could have shot a particular puddle of fake blood better by using a different camera lens. Or something. I tended to tune in and out when he talked.

I liked to rearrange Toby's DVDs to see if he noticed. He always noticed. They were organized on their white plastic shelf not by title but alphabetically by director's last name. I always said there was no way anyone could remember them all well enough to find what they were looking for. But, whenever he was searching for one of his favorite gore fests, Toby plucked it from the shelf in less than ten seconds.

After I was satisfied with my movie-shelf mayhem, I left Toby's isolation den and went into my parents' room. This little habit of mine, snooping while everyone was out, had sustained my curiosity about their lives since I was twelve or so. It made it so I didn't have to ask how their week had been; I already knew by the contents of their trash cans and which books had been removed from their nightstands.

The room was still warm and steamy, evidence of a recent shower in the connected bathroom. Dad had probably left for work minutes before I'd come through the door. I couldn't believe he wasn't tired of the night shift after all these years. Completely switching your sleep schedule to fry sugary carbs for a living? No, thank you. He'd stopped bringing me doughnut holes a long time ago. We'd never actually discussed it, but he somehow knew I wouldn't eat them anymore.

I opened Mom's closet and ran a hand along the shirts and sweaters inside. She spent so much time trying to look professional for her job running a teen homeless shelter in Cave Creek that she'd lost sight of herself as a woman. Most of these shirts were winter colors—forest green, magenta, black, navy blue—all long-sleeve and blousy. She wore them with khakis or black slacks and sensible, comfortable shoes. Mom and I were both slender and delicately boned. She could have done so much more with her wardrobe.

I walked out of their bedroom, down the stairs, and out the back door to the tool shed. The little shack had been on the property when my parents bought the house so they decided to leave it and store the few tools they owned inside. No one really used this place except me. It was unorganized, just a pile of pliers, hammers, and screwdrivers on a shelf against one wall. We didn't even own a lawn mower or any other large yard tools because my parents preferred to pay someone monthly for yard work rather than do it themselves. The floor of the shed was empty and covered in a layer of dust so thick that I could see my bare footprints when I moved. The walls had been painted red once, but the paint had a habit of falling off the wood in strips and curling up on the floor. I stepped on one of them and it crunched into hundreds of pieces under my toes. I grabbed a rusted pocketknife from the shelf of haphazard tools and headed outside and behind the shed.

"Hello, Twelve," I said to the squirrel. I'd left him out there that morning while Dad was still at work, two pushpins through each limb. He was stuck firmly into the hard earth so he couldn't escape. He was unconscious, probably hungry and dehydrated, but not yet dead.

I knelt beside Twelve and tapped his taut belly three times with my index finger. He snapped awake and started squeaking. I didn't know how they did it, but when they were in distress these squirrels seemed to not need to breathe. They just squeaked one continuous, impossibly high-pitched note. It wasn't very loud. No one besides me would be able to hear it, even if they had been right there in the backyard. If we had a dog, though, it would have lost its shit at the sound.

I worked a fingernail underneath the plastic part of one of the pins to loosen it from the ground. It made a little squishing sound as the point eased out of Twelve's paw by minuscule measurements. His shrieking became even more desperate.

"Oh, relax," I told him with the same tone I'd used on Alex an hour before. I almost said, "It's not like you're gonna die," but, well…

I gripped the pushpin between my thumb and forefinger and stroked the point across Twelve's belly. Gently. Gingerly. I started to press harder until I could hear it scraping against his skin. It wasn't smooth. The motion of the pin gathered Twelve's skin into an accordion pattern and skidded across it, creating tiny scratches at even intervals. A few drops of blood escaped his body, matting the fine fur of his underside. It surprised me every time that a pin anyone can buy at an office supply store, that my first grade teacher used to hang up our best assignments, could so easily eviscerate these tiny creatures.

I focused on his face then. Twelve squinted his eyes until the black beads could only be seen through tiny slits. He had stopped screaming. They always did eventually.

"All right, Twelve," I said. "Get ready." I pressed two fingers of my left hand against his rapidly beating heart. With my other hand, I stuck the pin into his stomach until the metal part couldn't be seen. The screeching came back. His heart rate increased.

I left the pin where it was and picked up the pocketknife. I fanned out the attachments, examining my options. Screwdriver, scissors, nail file, blade. The blade was thin and flimsy like it was made of a few layers of tinfoil. It didn't even seem sharp. I ran it against my palm and, sure enough, not even a mark. But it would be enough for this little guy.

Twelve finally started struggling, trying to break free. He used up so much power as he struggled through the pain of being staked to the ground, something I had seen several times with my squirrels. Seven had even summoned the adrenaline to tear one foot free, creating a clean rip between two toes about half an inch long. His limb would have been useless to help him escape, or to help him live if he did manage to break free, but he couldn't have known that with his tiny squirrel brain. They operated on instinct, not logic.

Twelve's struggling started to annoy me. Obviously, his fate was sealed and trying to get away was pointless. I jabbed him with the looks-like-tinfoil knife at the top of his belly and yanked, ripping a gaping hole in his gut. I kept my fingers pressed on his heart as it slowed and finally went still.

My fingertips were slick with rodent blood, turning my lime green nail polish an unsightly shade of vomit brown. I wiped as much of it as I could onto the dry parts of Twelve's fur, then removed the pins that had secured him to the ground and deposited them into the pocket of my jean skirt.

I examined the little corpse, jaggedly ripped open and spilling gore into the dirt. The miniature knife lay next to him, completing an artistic portrait of violence. If I'd had a camera, I would have taken a picture, but I probably would have been too tempted to share it. Something in the back of my mind told me that no one should know about this extracurricular activity.

I disposed of Twelve using my usual method: first into a plastic baggie, then a brown paper bag to be kept behind the toilet in my bathroom until the next time I left the house. The bundle would be tucked safely in my backpack until I could toss it into a public dumpster. I thought about all the famous serial killers who had tortured animals. Son of Sam, Dahmer, Bundy, BTK. Of course, most of them had graduated to torturing and killing humans by the time they were my age. I knew I was a little old, acting a little immaturely, to only have killed twelve rodents and a sick cat once by throwing a rock and knocking it from its perch on my backyard fence. I'd only meant to scare it, but whatever. It counted.

The difference between those long-gone boys and me was that they didn't necessarily start out expecting to take lives. I, on the other hand, was born in 1989, the year the US had more active serial killers than any other. I grew up hearing about the childhood serial killer behavior trifecta on the evening news: chronic bedwetting, pyromania, torturing animals. That list was polite dinner conversation. Everyone knew the signs, they just didn't see them in girls. I didn't wet the bed after I was potty trained, but I did revel in setting little fires whenever I was unsupervised. It was truly nothing but luck that prevented any of them from getting out of hand and revealing my secret.

What began as an impulse to destroy with fire shifted some time around puberty, becoming an impulse to cause pain. My first victim came about unexpectedly. Everyone thought our fifth-grade class guinea pig died of natural causes or old age, but they didn't know I had squeezed his fragile body with my soft, manicured hands until there was no more breath inside him. I felt such power and control from that unplanned act, I knew it couldn't be the last time.

The squirrels became a part of my routine after that. Every six months or so, whenever I felt the urge, I set up my dad's no-kill cage trap in the backyard and caught one. I strung it up all day while I was at school, then came home and killed it. I watched their beady eyes and felt their rapid hearts as they died. Then I disposed of them and went back to business as usual.

With Twelve safely in his hiding spot inside the double layer of bags, I turned on the shower and stripped out of my leotard and skirt. I stepped under the spray and washed off school, gymnastics practice, Alex, the walk home, and the last bits of Twelve's dried blood stuck under my fingernails. I shaved my legs and conditioned my hair twice. Just as the water started to cool, I twisted the knob and reached out from behind the cream-colored curtain to grab a towel from the rack.

After I had blown my hair dry and pulled on jeans and a plain pink t-shirt, the front door opened, and I heard Toby tumble inside. I smirked. Predictably, as soon as he entered his bedroom, he made his signature half-groan, half-growl sound and stomped down the hallway.

"Allegra!" he called. "Did you mess up my movies again?"

I popped my head out of my room before he made it all the way down the hall. I took a minute to notice that he was in the exact same Slipknot shirt and baggy black jeans he'd worn the day before and wondered whether he had slept in them. I also wondered if he'd bothered to change his underwear, but chances of that were low if he hadn't changed anything else.

"I sure did!" I shouted back. It was a kind of challenge. I was daring him to…I don't know, really. Hit me? Yell? It didn't matter. Love of horror movies aside, Toby had always been a gentle kid. He never would have verbally or physically punished me for picking on him. He probably wouldn't even tell Mom or Dad. I was willing to bet they didn't even know about the ongoing DVD migration project.

Toby made that sound again, then turned and huffed back to his room. I heard movie cases clicking against each other as he made sure to fix all the damage I had caused. I trotted downstairs and turned on the living room TV, wondering if Toby knew that I wouldn't mess with his things if his reactions didn't make it so much fun.

CHAPTER 2

Allegra

March 2007

Our school's dance team only had five members. Ashley, a pale red-headed freshman covered in freckles, was our newest member and the only current exception to the 'no freshmen on the varsity squad' rule because she had grown up dancing in an actual studio. She wore pointe shoes when she took ballet class outside of school and had the perfect figure and feet for it. The twins, Kaitlin and Karen, were impossible to tell apart ever since one cut her dark hair to match the other's pixie cut. They were seniors also, and I had admittedly always been a little jealous of how gorgeous they were. It wasn't a contest because I certainly never hurt for attention, but a white blonde just can't compete with mixed-race beauty. I'd never seen their dad so I wasn't sure what genes had mixed with their mother's Vietnamese features, but it seemed that they had gotten the best of both their parents' physical characteristics. The last team member, Yesenia, was a junior and the most athletic among us. She had a background in gymnastics and thought nothing of tumbling and twisting across the stage, always landing in the perfect 'ta-da!' position.

And then there was me. I was flexible enough, graceful enough, and dependable enough to be on the varsity dance team without letting any of these traits stand out too far. I wasn't the best at tumbling like Yesenia. I didn't have the best technique like Ashley. I wasn't the first to draw the audience's eye with my beauty like Kaitlin and Karen. As in the rest of my life, I had intentionally placed myself directly in the middle of the pack.

Once a year, our team traveled to a dance convention to mingle with dancers from across the country and take classes from master teachers. Our coach, Andrea, had grown up in a dance studio like Ashley and felt it was important to get exposure to other teachers in a more 'traditional' setting. I think Andrea's greatest regret was teaching a high school dance team instead of real dance classes. But, she was pushing sixty and worked wherever she could find work. My mom once muttered that *that's what you get when you pick a major like dance in college*, which I didn't think was quite fair. It wasn't like teaching dance came with a 401K and retirement plan. Being a dance teacher was like freelancing; you got to make your own schedule, but the hustle to find enough work to pay the bills was tough when there wasn't a single company scheduling you for forty hours a week. That's how Andrea explained it to us once when Ashley asked what kinds of Careers (she emphasized the word so you could hear the capital C) we could expect to find if we chose to pursue dance in the real world.

This year's convention was called SparkleDance! and was held at a hotel in downtown Phoenix. Last year we flew to Georgia for some equally ridiculously named event, but this one was driving distance from our school in Mesa, Arizona. Even though we had to pay for dance team trips ourselves, I couldn't help but wonder if something had changed with the school's travel budget or Andrea's work schedule to prompt the downsizing. I thought the point was to get out of our natural habitat, not drive forty minutes up the freeway.

Even though we were staying inside our own county, the team did get to leave school at noon on a Friday and drive over, then stay in the hotel for two nights. It was still a mini vacation, and the parent chaperone was not one of mine. This particular vacation was coming at just the right time since it would have been my first Friday afternoon without Alex.

Along with Andrea, the other adult chaperone was Ashley's mom, Sarah. She looked like a taller clone of her daughter, almost down to the placement of their freckles. The group met in our school's parking lot after the final lunch bell rang and everyone piled into Sarah's enormous red van. Once we got on the road, Sarah and Andrea, sitting shotgun, started chatting about the current real estate market. I'd tried to grab a window seat but ended up between the twins in the middle row. Behind us, Yesenia and Ashley chattered about brands of dance clothing. Yesenia wouldn't stop popping her gum.

"Did you look at the convention schedule online?" Either Kaitlin or Karen asked me, startling me out of my mild trance.

"Not too closely, but I know I want to take that contemporary class tomorrow morning."

"We do too! I love anything you can do barefoot," the same twin answered. Her sister nodded in agreement.

"Know what I'm *not* looking forward to, though?" Ashley chimed in from the back seat. "The full-group warm-up first thing in the morning. Sorry, but nobody wants to sweat in a room with two hundred people at eight a.m. I'll be awake, but I won't be, like, *awake*, ya know?"

"Will that be better or worse than tap class, do you think?" Yesenia asked. She popped her gum again. I wished she would just choke on it already.

Ashley groaned and rolled her eyes. "Ugh. Better. Nothing is worse than tap class. I won't take it, and they can't make me." She crossed her arms emphatically.

Andrea turned around, her long, dyed-black hair falling over her shoulder. "Remember, girls," she said to all of us. "We need to agree on at least one class to take as a group each day. These trips are about team bonding as well as learning new things."

"Is that why we don't get our own rooms?" Yesenia asked, smirking.

Sarah let out a tinkling giggle from the driver's seat, studiously keeping her eyes on the road. "No, that's because hotel rooms are expensive."

Andrea joined her laughter. "*And* for team bonding. Anyway, it's not like we're cramming the seven of us into one room. We have three, two beds in each. I also called ahead and made sure they have rollaway beds. You guys can pick your own roommates."

"Ashley and I don't mind sharing a queen size," Sarah said. I glanced back at Ashley who just shrugged. I couldn't tell if she actually minded. I had been wanting to ask her if it was hard being the baby of the group, her mom always tagging along to our activities, but couldn't foresee a time when that wouldn't be an awkward question.

We pulled into the hotel parking lot a little after one o'clock, and it was already packed. Sarah found a spot in the farthest corner from the entrance, and we all piled out and retrieved our overnight bags from the back of the van. The check-in line in the lobby was at least twenty people long. Most of them were groups of girls in matching jackets, chaperoned by one or two adults. Our team jackets were either tucked away in our bags or at home because it was March in Phoenix and the temperature was already rapidly approaching 100 degrees, so no one knew who we were. That was just as well. We'd found out before that school dance teams were treated differently than 'real' dancers at conventions and competitions. The studio dancers equated us with cheerleaders, and they did *not* respect cheerleaders. Even so, I wished I was wearing my purple and gray team jacket to proudly proclaim that we were a school dance team, not studio snobs.

When it was our turn to check in, Andrea gave the clerk her name, and he gave us three envelopes with room numbers on the front and keys inside. He also informed us that our rooms were connected to one another so we could travel between them without going into the hallway.

"That's so cool!" Yesenia exclaimed like she'd never been to a hotel before. I rolled my eyes.

We took the elevator as a group to the fifth floor. When the doors opened, a giggly group of girls about our age exited, and we took their place inside. Their team jackets were black and orange, announcing to the world that they were also a high school dance team. *Oilers Varsity Dance Team! Huntington Beach, CA. Class of 2008.* The last member of their team to leave the elevator wore heavy black eye makeup and held my gaze a little longer than a stranger should. She had spiky black hair and wore a black leotard and red cotton shorts under her unzipped jacket. The red clashed with her orange jacket in a surprisingly satisfying way. Her bare legs were pink and covered in goosebumps from the air-conditioned hotel. Seeing them brought my attention to the fact that I had been freezing since we stepped inside. For some reason I wanted to tell this girl that we were alike even though I had no idea whether that was true. I could have had as little in common with her as I did with my own teammates; I just felt this connection, like an invisible string pulling me toward her. Then the elevator doors closed, snapping the tether, and we all ascended to the fifth floor.

We had just enough time to drop our bags in our rooms (I would be rooming with Yesenia) before it was time to go back down the elevators and check in for the convention. SparkleDance! was hosting a combination mixer/registration/dance party event for all the students, participants, and instructors that would be starting any minute. Our group arrived in the long, carpeted hallway leading to the ballrooms just in time to see the early birds let in through a pair of large, white double doors. We followed them in to find the overhead lights dimmed and colored disco balls projecting rotating squares of color onto the walls. Pop music played at a deafening volume. Convention employees energetically walked the perimeter of the room encouraging us to get on the dance floor or socialize and make new friends. I refrained from both, opting to sit in a chair at the side of the room and watch the madness.

I saw the girl in red shorts again when the party was almost over. She seemed to be having the time of her life on the dance floor with her fellow Oilers, jumping and spinning aimlessly like a toddler. She even showed off with a handstand and a few one-handed cartwheels. I couldn't stop watching her. She was performing moves that would have looked ridiculous on anyone else, but she delivered them with an effortless grace that can't be taught. The magic spell was broken when she humanized herself by filling a paper cup with water from one of the dispensers positioned around the room's perimeter, then accidentally spilling it down the front of her leotard. She jumped and shimmied from the shock of the cold. I couldn't hear her, but her gaping smile told me that she was laughing loudly. She didn't see me smiling across the dark room. I could tell that she was used to getting looks from strangers, so she wasn't paying attention to whose eyes might be following her. I knew this because I carried myself the same way.

On Saturday, the morning workout in the same giant ballroom was halfway over before I noticed Red Shorts Girl was warming up just a few feet away from me. The room was much more crowded than the previous night for the mixer. I estimated the number to be around three hundred, including the parents and teachers sitting in chairs against the wall instead of participating in the warm-up.

After leading everyone in slow stretches and some light cardio from a stage at the front of the room, the instructor told everyone to take a water break and put her microphone down next to the sound system. Red Shorts Girl walked toward me on her way to get water. We made eye contact, and I smiled the smile that strangers give each other in passing. Instead of just letting her walk away again, I spoke.

"I love your hair. How do you get it to spike like that?"

She laughed and replied, "Lots of gel."

I nodded as if I'd ever used gel in my life. "It looks awesome. I would cut my hair that short if I was guaranteed it would look like yours."

"No way. Yours is gorgeous, you have to own it!"

My hand shot up to grasp the messy bun I'd thrown my hair into a few minutes before class began. "How can you even tell? It's tied up, and plus, I'm all sweaty."

She shrugged. "The rest of you is gorgeous, so I just assumed."

I blushed mildly, and then mentally reprimanded myself. *You're blushing? You're blushing? Screw that, you're Allegra. You're the beautiful, brazen girl who makes boys blush. You're not the boy who blushes.* I recovered my confidence and smiled in a way I hoped was mildly mysterious. "I'm Allegra, by the way. What's your name?"

"Nova." She held her hand out for a shake, and it felt natural instead of being cloaked in awkwardness the way it usually was when I shook hands with another teenager. "I'm from California. Where'd you come from?"

"Oh, really close by. I live in Mesa, it's about forty-five minutes from here."

"Nice. You staying in the hotel?"

"I am, actually. I'm here with my school dance team."

"Me too!" *I know,* I wanted to say, but couldn't think of how to word it without sounding like a stalker. Instead of saying anything, I just nodded and smiled.

We got our water and finished the group warm-up. The group of hundreds broke up into smaller classes for the second session of the day. Before I lost track of her again, I caught Nova gently by the arm.

"Hey," I said cautiously. "Do you have lunch plans?"

"Well, I'm supposed to meet up with my group…"

"So am I. But I don't really feel like it."

She smiled with lots of teeth. "Suddenly I don't either. Meet me in the lobby after the second class?"

I nodded. "Sure. See you then." I gave her forearm a light squeeze before letting go, and watched her walk away.

Meeting Nova in the lobby was a blur. We bought sandwiches wrapped in plastic and bottled juice from a small refrigerated section of the hotel gift shop, then took them up to her room. She was sharing with two other girls from her group, but she knew they'd be going to a restaurant for lunch and wouldn't be back to the room before afternoon classes began. In the elevator on the way up, she found a way to mention that she was bi, because that's what bi girls did when they met a girl they thought was cute. I briefly let myself wonder why they did this when sometimes all I had to do was accidentally look at a guy too long and he wanted to hook up with me.

We set our sandwiches and drinks on one of the tables and ignored them. She switched the TV on, but we ignored that too. I sat next to her on the bed. She put her whole hand on the back of my neck, palms to fingertips. It was cold from her juice bottle, and I wanted it to stay there forever. I leaned forward and kissed her on the mouth. Nothing was a blur anymore. I could feel the whole scene with perfect clarity.

After a few minutes, once she realized I wasn't going to run scared like other straight girls had probably done to her, she scooted up to the head of the bed and patted the spot next to her. Instead, I climbed on top and kissed my way down her collarbone and chest until I reached the V of her leotard neckline. Somehow her fingertips were everywhere on my body at once. I used my left hand to hold my body up over hers, and the right to trace her exposed neck and shoulders with two slow fingers. *If I were a vampire*, I thought, *I could bite and exsanguinate in no time at all. As I am, I could use just a little more pressure and stop her breathing before she could fight back.*

Nova unexpectedly flipped us both over in one gesture, and suddenly she was on top. She had sensed that I had all the power and was intentionally taking it back. I'd pulled that move enough times to recognize it. For the first time, it didn't feel wrong not to be in control. I trusted this stranger for some reason.

"I noticed you yesterday in the elevator, you know." Nova stopped kissing me and shifted her body so it was next to mine on the bed.

"I did not know," I replied. This wasn't a lie. I'd been too busy noticing her. Admitting this would have given away too much power in a situation where she already had the upper hand, so I went with a slight subject change. "I saw you dancing last night."

"Everyone was dancing last night. It's a dance convention."

"I know. I mean…at the mixer. You were—" I cut myself off because I couldn't believe I was tripping over my words. After letting out a frustrated huff, I started the sentence over again. "I was watching you freestyle with your friends. It looked like you were having fun."

She gifted me with a genuine grin. "I was. It was a cool party. The classes this morning weren't too bad either." I didn't respond. "You're a wallflower, aren't you?"

"I guess. What do you mean?"

"Well, if you were watching me then you weren't dancing yourself. Why?"

"I just like to watch. Try to figure out what people are thinking by studying their faces." I didn't know why I kept telling her the truth. She had already broken through my carefully constructed middle-of-the-pack approach to life and identified me as an outsider.

"Oh, yeah? What am I thinking right now?" She transformed her face to an exaggeratedly pensive expression, like she was trying to solve world hunger or one of the great unsolvable math problems.

My own face broke into a grin. "Not like that, I'm not psychic!"

"Like what, then?"

"I just… Okay. There's this word I like. Sonder. It means every single person you see has a life that's just as three-dimensional and complex as your own. Everyone has a story, even if they're only a part of yours for the five seconds it took to walk past them. When I people-watch, I'm wondering what their story is."

"You could ask them."

"That would take the mystery out of it."

Nova suddenly bounced off the bed, got her cell phone out of a zippered compartment in her black dance bag, and checked the time. "The first afternoon class is about to start. Are you at all interested in—" she consulted a printed schedule retrieved from the same pocket, "—beginning-slash-intermediate tap?"

"I couldn't be less interested," I said, stretching out until only my fingertips touched the head of the bed and my bare toes almost reached the foot.

"Neither could I." She climbed back onto the bed. "Whatever will we do to pass the time?"

I put my palm on the back of her neck, mimicking hers on me when we first entered the room. Without waiting for her to breathe, I kissed her. Eased her lips apart with my tongue. Turned her onto her back and hovered over her, thinking again how easy it would be to squeeze her throat until she stopped breathing. She'd think it was a sexy game at first. By the time she tried to tap out, she'd already be too weak to fight back. I disconnected our mouths and laid my fingers on what I imagined would be the perfect spot.

"Have you ever been choked during sex?" I asked.

"No."

"Have you ever been cut during sex?"

"No."

"Have you ever cut *yourself*?"

"Like…" She looked uncomfortable, but stared straight into my eyes when she answered, "Yeah."

"Did you want to die?"

"Why else would I have cut myself?"

I shrugged. Waited. Watched.

"And to answer your first two questions, I've never had sex," she confessed.

"Oh yeah, me neither." I wave my hand like it's no big deal.

"You're lying."

"Yes, I am."

"I'm not."

"I know."

"I do like you, though."

"I know." I didn't want to tell her the truth anymore, but it bubbled up and out of my mouth before I could stop it. "I like you too."

"We'll never see each other again after this weekend," she told me.

"You're probably right."

"Should we be friends on Facebook at least?"

"Wouldn't that ruin the mystery of this whole encounter?"

"You're so caught up with the mystery of things. Anyway, my shrink always tells me not to answer a question with a question."

I smiled with half my mouth. "Look at all these new things I'm learning about you, Nova. Now I know you see a shrink."

She shrugged. "I'm a depressed teen whose parents found out she self-injures. Where else would I spend my Friday afternoons?"

"Look," I said, my sudden seriousness even surprising myself. "I don't know your story, but I know you have one. And I can tell you're fucking cool, and smart, and… You're just not like anyone I've met before." I kissed her then because otherwise I would have kept going. *I don't want today to be the only time we ever see each other*, I wanted to say. Even though I didn't verbalize it, I think she saw this desire in my eyes.

"Allegra." She looked down at her lap when she said my name. Like a prayer or a meditation chant. After too long, she continued. "What's your last name? I'm gonna add you on Facebook."

"Long," I gave in. "Allegra Long. My middle name's not listed."

"What is it?"

"Elizabeth."

I stood up, collected my sandwich and juice from the desk, and picked up my dance bag from the floor. She stood up and followed me to the door where she kissed me one more time, hand on the back of my neck, before I opened it and left her room.

Back downstairs in the ballrooms, I found Andrea and Sarah watching the tap class from chairs at the side of the room. Ashley sat at their legs in the splits, no doubt limbering up for the ballet barre class that was next. Yesenia, Kaitlin, and Karen were doing their best to keep up with the instructor's directions, shuffling in their flip flops or bare feet because none of us owned tap shoes.

"Where were you at lunch?" Ashley asked.

"Yeah, did you eat? We waited for you before heading to the restaurant," her mom added.

I held up my sandwich, now room temperature and probably inedible. "I was exploring the hotel. Sorry I didn't check in."

"It's okay, I just want to make sure I don't lose any of you girls," Andrea said with a smile. "Let me know if you want to 'explore' alone again. Maybe we'll implement the buddy system for safety."

I hoped she was kidding.

The tap teacher gave the class a water break, and our remaining three joined the group long enough to sip from their plastic bottles.

"This is torture," Yesenia whined. "How much longer?"

"Eternity," either Kaitlin or Karen responded. "We will never be finished taking this class. It will never end. We'll all die here."

"It has to end eventually. Ballet is next!" Ashley alternated her split so her left leg was in front.

The teacher called the class back to the floor. Yesenia groaned, and the three of them dutifully returned to finish the class. I plopped down next to Ashley and did some half-hearted floor stretches. I watched the entrance of the ballroom until I saw Nova come in. She caught my eye and smiled. I winked discreetly back. In my stomach, the butterflies I'd always thought must be dead, if they had ever been there at all, woke up and fluttered wildly.

For the first time since meeting up with her in the lobby, I realized the difference between hooking up with Nova and sleeping with Alex and the rest. The boys had been distractions, ways out of the numbness inside my head or excuses to have orgasms. Nova was something else entirely. I would probably still be thinking about her for days or weeks afterward. I would be waiting to see her name pop up in my friend request box on Facebook. She actually made me *feel* something. Not only that, but she made me want to be honest. This was brand new.

CHAPTER 3

Allegra

April 2007

"You go to that school?"

I looked up from *To Kill a Mockingbird* and studied the face of the boy at the next table. He was blonde, sturdy, muscled. Probably a frat boy with an empty head and a deep love affair with kegs.

"What?" I asked.

"I said, do you go to that school across the street?" He pointed to what was, in fact, my high school.

"Yep."

"Oh, nice. You must be a senior, right? You eighteen?"

I wasn't about to strike up a conversation with some random douchebag in Starbucks. I sort of half-shrugged and looked pointedly back at my book.

"What does that mean?" the boy asked. "You don't know how old you are?"

I sighed and set *To Kill a Mockingbird* on the table in front of me. "No. It means I don't want to tell *you* how old I am, or anything else about myself. I'm just sitting here."

"Yeah, sitting there looking gorgeous."

"And now I'm moving." I gathered my backpack, book, and iced latte and walked to a table at the other end of the cafe. I didn't know why I wasn't flirting back with this idiot. He could have been of some use to me, I'm sure. But it was only a week since my encounter with Nova, and two days since she'd friended me on Facebook, and I just wasn't in the mood to be ogled by a strange man. But lucky me, he followed.

"So, do you want to go out with me some time?" He waggled his eyebrows and leaned on the back of a chair with both fists.

"I don't even know you." It was something I knew normal girls would say, so I said it.

"I know how to change that. I'm Chad. Let me get your number, huh?"

Of course his name was Chad. Had there ever been a boy who looked and acted like him whose name *wasn't* Chad?

"Okay, here's what's going to happen." I put my things down on my new table and ran my fingers through my hair. "I'm going to sit down and continue to drink my coffee. Alone. And you're gonna go back to whatever you were doing before you started following me around this place."

"Or we can get out of here together. How about going for a walk with me?"

"No! Are you stupid?"

"Come on, sweetheart. I'm just trying to tell you you're beautiful."

"Listen, asshole. Lay off or I'll fucking kill you!"

He put his hands up in mock submission. "Whoa, now."

I heard another voice from behind me. "You guys doing okay over here?" It was one of the baristas, carrying a tray in one hand and a rag in the other.

"Yeah, thanks," Frat Boy muttered, waving her away.

"Oh," I said before the girl could leave. "Don't you want to harass her, too? She's pretty." She was, in fact, attractive in an Ally-Sheedy-in-the-last-scene-of-*The-Breakfast-Club* way. Her sharp nose and chin gave her face an interesting angular look, and her dark eyes made me think of the chocolate diamond earrings I had received on my sixteenth birthday but not yet worn.

"Whoa, now," Frat Boy said again. "Who's harassing? I'm just saying, you should let me take you on a date." Then, he had the fucking nerve to take a hank of my hair between his index and middle fingers and hold it for several excruciating seconds before tucking it behind my ear. His palm brushed my shoulder on the way down. The barista just watched, shock etched into her frozen features.

"Okay, we're done here." I gathered my belongings and stormed away. Once outside, I took a minute to put my book into my backpack and take a couple of deep breaths. As I zipped up my bag, I felt someone approach me from behind. *Oh great*, I thought, *Chad's back.* I wondered again why I wasn't playing along with this jerk. He was what Alex would grow up to be, after all, and he probably had at least one thing that would benefit me if I played along. Money, a car, friends with connections or fake IDs, or at least rich parents with a stocked liquor cabinet.

Okay, I decided, *what the hell?* I put on an apologetic half-smile and got ready to be called a fickle bitch once, and only once, before being forgiven and probably touched again. But when I turned around, it was the barista who stood before me.

"Hey," she said, still holding her tray. "Are you okay? I told that guy to leave and then I made sure he did, so you can come back inside if you want."

I turned my fake apologetic smile meant for Frat Boy into a genuine and grateful one for this girl. It hadn't occurred to me until she said this how much I *didn't* want to give in to Chad just because he was relentless. That was how I'd ended up with Alex, and with at least five or six boys before Alex. Until she had sent another potential away, I hadn't considered that sending them away was even a possibility.

"Oh. Um, thanks. This might be a stupid question for someone who works at Starbucks, but can I buy you a coffee as a thank you?"

She looked surprised for a split second before returning my smile. "I'm in the middle of unpacking some things in the back, but I get my lunch break in about an hour. Will you still be around?"

I checked my watch, which I guess was stupid because I already knew I had no plans that afternoon and wasn't expected home at any particular time. It was a little after three p.m.

"Yeah," I answered. "I'll still be here."

"Great. I'm Robin, by the way."

"I'm Allegra." I paused, considering my next sentence before letting it out. "If you want, you can call me Ally."

I didn't see Robin again until four when she emerged from the staff area, brunette bangs stuck to her forehead with a thin layer of sweat. I wondered if she'd been unpacking something light, like travel cups, or fifty-pound bags of coffee beans. I wondered if Starbucks even ordered their coffee beans in bags that large. Then, I wondered why I was wondering all these things that didn't affect me at all.

When she sat down at my table, she already had a freshly made Venti Iced Something and one of the lunches in a clear plastic box from the refrigerated shelves by the checkout counter.

"Hey, I was supposed to buy you a coffee for rescuing me from that creep," I said goodnaturedly.

"All in a day's work, ma'am." She lowered the register of her voice several octaves to imitate an old-fashioned cop. Talking like that made her lips purse involuntarily, which made me laugh.

"So, Robin, what do you do when you're not saving the day?"

"Pretty much this." She gestured around the Starbucks lobby. "I got promoted to full-time a few months ago, so I basically live here now."

"You don't go to school?"

"Graduated high school last year. I've been thinking about college, but it's so expensive. I don't want to go until I really know what I want to do with my life."

I nodded. That explained why I hadn't seen her around the hallways. "What about you, Ally?"

"What about me, what?" I didn't mean to sound defensive. It must have been a reflex. Luckily, she didn't seem phased by my tone.

"Well, I heard you tell Creepo that you go to the school across the street. High school can't take up all your time. What do you like to do?"

"Weirdly, it kind of does. I'm on the dance team so we have a lot of practices after school and sometimes on weekends. Actually, last weekend we went to this convention in Phoenix to take master classes and stuff. I met—" Right at that moment I realized that I wasn't ready to tell anyone about Nova yet. I still wasn't even sure what the encounter meant to me. "—some pretty cool people," I finished lamely.

"That's awesome! That you're involved in that, I mean. I wish I'd partic- ipated in more stuff when I was in high school. Anime club doesn't count. I wasn't even into Anime, but the girl I had a crush on was the vice president. I thought joining would turn her gay and make her fall in love with me."

I laughed again. Robin smiled too, in a self-deprecating way.

"Whatever happened to her?" I asked.

"She's married to some dude now and pregnant, I think. It *has* been ten whole months since graduation, so it's about time."

"Oh, yeah. I'm surprised she waited this long," I said sarcastically. "What's stopping you from doing the same thing?"

She shrugged. "I dunno. I guess I've never really seen myself settling down with a guy even though I do date them sometimes. And gay mar- riage isn't legal."

"Oh yeah, that pesky law." This time, we laughed together.

Robin and I spent all thirty minutes of her lunch break talking. She told me about the worst customer she'd had that day (surprisingly not Chad), and I told her about the quiz I'd failed earlier, given unexpectedly by my most obnoxious teacher. She didn't ask if I liked girls, and I didn't volunteer the information one way or the other because I honestly wasn't sure if Nova had been a fluke. Was I bi now? Gay? The instant chemistry with Nova, coupled with my resistance from Chad and how badly I didn't want Robin's lunch break to end made me think maybe I was somewhere on that spectrum.

Then again, maybe I was just starved for friends since I'd never had many. I didn't count the girls on the dance team as friends, just acquain- tances I was forced to hang out with in order to perform my chosen extra- curriculars. I didn't hate them, just wouldn't invite them over to bake cookies and sing '80s jams into our hairbrushes. I'd never needed friends before, but maybe I was eight years early with my quarter-life crisis and suddenly starved for human attention.

Before she went back to work, Robin put her number into my cell phone. I called her while she sat across from me, and when my number popped up on her phone, she saved it.

"I'll text you when I get off, okay? Maybe we can hang out this weekend." She said this like it was no big deal. Maybe it wasn't. I didn't know how having friends worked.

"Yeah," I said, trying to keep any hint of sarcasm or flirtation out of my voice because I wasn't yet sure where I wanted to fit her into my life. "That would be fun."

I took the bus home. "It's me!" I yelled when I walked through the front door.

"Hey, Ally!" I was shocked that my customary greeting to no one actually got a response. It was Toby, sprawled out on the living room couch with a plate of cut-up PB&J sandwich pieces balanced on his stomach. At fourteen, Toby was capable of cooking whatever he wanted but lazy enough that he basically lived off of peanut butter and jelly unless Mom made him something else.

"What are you watching?" I asked him.

"The original *Halloween*."

"Why is that on in April?"

He grinned up at me. "It's not. I had it saved on the TiVo."

"Do you ever consider watching something other than B-level horror movies?"

"They're not all bad. What's with all the questions, anyway?"

"Nothing, just curious."

I was going to ask him if Mom was home because I'd forgotten to notice whether her car was in the driveway, but that would have been just been another question. I wandered upstairs to my room, thinking about how that was probably the longest conversation Toby and I had had that year. Since he started high school and found the other members of the Scaredy Cat Club, an ironically named organization he started for other horror movie buffs, he hadn't been bored or lonely enough to pretend we have anything in common.

Upstairs, the house felt as cold and sterile as a surgery theater. The white carpet had been vacuumed recently, haphazard tracks still showing. The porcelain, plastic, and glass in the bathroom all gleamed. In my parents' room, the bed was made perfectly and there was nothing on the floor that shouldn't have been. A framed picture of Toby and I laughing at the camera, ages four and eight, sat on top of Mom's dresser. Dad must have gone on a cleaning binge before leaving for work that afternoon. The area felt more like a museum than a family home. This was fitting since, between Mom and Dad's opposing work schedules, my dance and school, and whatever Toby spent his extra time doing, I couldn't remember the last time we'd all been home at the same time.

With Toby here, I couldn't visit the tool shed without arousing suspicion. I didn't have a critter waiting for me that day anyway. I entered my own room and plopped onto the bed, kicking off my shoes before they could hit the purple, swirl-patterned bedspread. For a few minutes, I let myself think about Nova. Her exposed neck. How easy it would have been. Poking a squirrel with pins and rusty knives could never compare to taking a human life.

Then again, I had no proof that killing her would have been easy. She could have been unexpectedly strong and fought me off. Even if I'd managed to choke the life out of her, I would have had to decide whether to leave the body there to be discovered by one of her teammates or a hotel maid, or try to dispose of it. Disposal could get messy, especially in a hotel where everything is freshly laundered and white and there were no tools or chemicals at my disposal. A human was too large to stick in a baggie and toss in the nearest dumpster. No, killing someone in a hotel would be much less than ideal. I'd have to come up with a solid plan. I was glad that things with Nova ended the way they did. I was sure that my opportunity to kill someone would arise organically. Maybe it would be Robin. She seemed like a sweet, genuine person who would never see it coming.

A revelation hit me like a truck: it could have been Chad! I could have flirted back, agreed to go somewhere with him, and somehow lured him over a cliff or into a car accident. I would have been willing to risk an injury myself if it meant he died at my hands. Then again, I wanted to kill him with my *hands*. I wanted to feel the knife penetrate his skin and rip a clean line through his flesh. I wanted my fingers securely pressed to his jugular vein, pulsing with blood until it slowed to a full stop. What I wanted would take much more planning. It was okay that I let Chad get away. Disposable boys were everywhere.

About an hour later while I stared at my laptop screen, zoning out on my Economics homework, the front door opened and closed. Mom's sensible shoes squeaked from the entryway, where she dropped something heavy, probably her bag, to the living room. She greeted Toby, her voice getting increasingly louder as she moved closer to the stairs. Once she had climbed them, she poked her head into my doorway.

"Hey there. How was school today?" Her blouse was wrinkled at the bottom, one side untucked from her khaki slacks. I noticed a few grays sneaking through the barrier of copper-colored hair dye she used to avoid the appearance that she was aging.

"It was fine," I told her. "Hung out at Starbucks for a while afterward. Mr. Berry is making us read *To Kill A Mockingbird* again even though we all told him we read it as freshmen."

"Ah. Well, maybe you'll have a different perspective on it now that you're older and wiser."

"Are you using your work voice on me?"

Mom paused and thought about it for a few seconds. "I guess I am, yeah. Sorry about that. It's hard to turn it off, you know?"

I laughed a little. I didn't mind, honestly. Working with homeless and otherwise underprivileged youth all day had actually made her pretty good at talking to Toby and me about things like why we have to go to school and become functioning members of society.

"What do you want for dinner?" she asked.

"I don't care." I really didn't. The caffeine from two iced lattes was still coursing through my veins and tricking my metabolism into thinking I didn't need to eat dinner.

"Want to do something easy, like pizza? I'm too tired to cook."

"That sounds good," I said.

She nodded, satisfied, left my doorway, and continued down the hall to her bedroom. She closed the door, probably hoping for a little alone time to unwind from work before coming back out to face more teenagers. I put my laptop down on the bed and closed it, vowing to finish the assignment later. I wasn't worried. I'd never turned in homework late in my life. I was just about to grab my backpack and consult my planner to see what else was due soon when Toby's quick little footsteps hustled up the stairs.

He took Mom's place in my doorway. He was dressed in all black from hoodie to shoes. His hair was dyed black too. Was I the only person in this family who was satisfied with their natural hair color? He shook his long, straight bangs out of his eyes before he spoke. "Hey, I'm about to start another movie. Want to watch?"

"Which one is it?"

"That one that came out last year, *The Hamiltons*. I heard it has a big gruesome murder scene in a slaughterhouse. I went to that used bookstore with the movie club after school and found the DVD for five dollars!"

I smiled at his childlike excitement. "Is it real-life scary and gross, or supernatural?"

"Supernatural, I think. My friend told me it also has a vampire family or something."

"Hmm… I do love a good family drama. I'm in." I stood up and followed Toby downstairs where the DVD was already cued up to the opening credits.

Eventually, Mom came downstairs in her sweatpants and asked what we wanted on our pizza. When it came, the three of us ate on the couch while we watched the Hamilton siblings make ill-fated decisions based on their uncontrollable bloodlust. If you squinted, it was almost like our family was used to spending time together. As the end credits rolled, my cell phone vibrated in my pocket. I took it out and flipped it open to a text from Robin. We made plans to get lunch the next day before she started her afternoon shift at Starbucks. The butterflies that had made their first appearance exactly a week before fluttered in my gut once again. I didn't know if she'd be my first victim or just my first actual friend, but I couldn't wait to find out.

CHAPTER 4

Robin

May 2006

The traffic light switched from red to green, and I removed my foot from the brake pedal of my dad's pickup truck. I eased back up to the speed limit of fifty-five, then pushed past it until I was cruising at seventy. I knew this road so well. I would circle this one stretch of road until I got sleepy. Get on the freeway, drive a few miles, exit and turn around, and get back on the freeway until the exit that leads to my neighborhood. I always kept the windows open, even if it started to rain. Sometimes I drove until one or two in the morning. Then I'd stumble into the house, windblown and red-eyed, drop the keys back into the bowl near the door, and go to bed.

Dad understood. He never complained when I used half a tank of gas in one night. I don't know where he thought I went, but what mattered was that he trusted me. Sometimes I liked to look at pictures my Bubbe, his mom, had taken of him in the '80s. The state of his own hair and eyes in those pictures told me that even though we were separated by a couple of decades, we weren't all that different. Those pictures also reminded me how lucky I was to have inherited my half-Japanese, half-Caucasian mother's thin, straight hair texture; if I'd been blessed with Dad's Jewfro, there was no way that quickly running a brush through my hair would eliminate most of the evidence of my late-night drives.

I turned right onto a side street and my headlights brought attention to a bicyclist's reflectors. I kept to the left and wondered what someone was doing out on a bike at midnight, wearing shorts and no helmet in the misty dark. Were they running from something? Did they have to leave so quickly that changing into warm clothes hadn't been an option? Or was this really the time of night they chose to exercise?

On this particular night, I was feeling extra disheartened because I'd finally finished the blanket I had been working on for months. I had just woven in the final loose end of yarn when Dad came into my room to say goodnight around eleven. The tightly coiled curls of his hair were disheveled and his beard looked lopsided like he'd fallen asleep on the couch after dinner and was only now getting up to go to bed. He had sleep in his eyes. I was jealous.

I did take a few minutes to admire the finished blanket. I'd recently mastered the mitered square and was now obsessed with using the pattern whenever possible. The blanket was large enough to cover my entire queen-size bed. Each twelve-inch square had taken about an hour to complete. There was only one mistake in the first square, and no one would notice it except me. Looking at the blanket made me feel like an artist. I folded it in half and laid it carefully on my bed, then grabbed Dad's keys and locked the door behind me on the way out.

Now it was past midnight and I was still driving in circles waiting for my eyelids to get heavy. The lights outside the truck were starting to blur, which was a good sign. "Come on," I said out loud to my body. "I have school tomorrow. Just give me a little sleep." I exited the freeway and got into the left turn lane. The upcoming light switched to yellow. I wouldn't be able to make it through before it turned to red, so I slowed down. When it turned green again, I gunned it as fast as possible to the next light, left turn signal flashing my intention to get back on the freeway at the next entrance.

Suddenly, a woman in a black hoodie and dark pants darted into the street. I jabbed the horn in the center of the steering wheel, warning her that I was coming as if my headlights weren't a good enough clue. She either didn't realize I was so close or thought she could make it across in time. I really thought I wouldn't intersect her path. She kept going. I kept going. When I finally slammed on my brakes, it was because the impact of her body on the hood of Dad's pickup shocked my own body into emergency mode. I think I screamed.

We were on a small side street, and no other headlights threatened to illuminate what I had done. "Holy shit, holy shit, holy shit," I kept saying as I got out of the car and approached her.

The woman lay close to the curb. She wasn't moving. One of her legs was at an impossible angle. I could tell it was broken. Other than that, she looked okay. I couldn't see any blood, either because there wasn't any or because we weren't directly under a streetlight and her clothes were dark. I focused on her face. She was maybe ten years older than me. She wore a full face of makeup including fake eyelashes and lipstick. Her eyeliner came to perfect points at the corners. I saw pain in her brown eyes. I sat on the curb staring at her in shock as her breathing became more labored. Maybe she was suffering from something more serious than a broken leg. I was too scared to move from my perch on the curb. Definitely too scared to touch her. She still hadn't moved, but she wouldn't stop looking at me.

After what seemed like an hour but was probably only a few minutes, the girl tried to lift her head. Her mouth screwed into a grimace of effort and pain. From the new angle, I saw blood dripping down the back of her neck. That meant a serious head injury. She tried to talk and a tiny amount of blood leaked out of her mouth. That meant internal injuries. Images of broken ribs with jagged edges poking into her organs lodged themselves in my brain and refused to be shaken away. She was still breathing. I was still frozen.

I don't know how long I sat on the curb silently watching blood and life seep from her body. The time finally came when her painted lips went still. Her chest stopped rising and falling. It was quieter without the sound of her breathing. She was gone.

Eventually, I used the emergency flashlight Dad had insisted I keep in my glove compartment for emergencies to check the front of the truck for damages. Not even a scratch.

"How is that possible?" I wondered aloud. I had literally killed someone with this weapon of a vehicle and you couldn't even tell.

The fear hit me all at once. The only word in my head was *dead*. She was dead. I killed her. I killed her with my Dad's perfectly unblemished truck. I would get arrested. There would be a trial. I would go to prison.

I couldn't do that to Dad. Couldn't leave him like Mom did when I was too small to even remember her.

I let my body's sometimes-convenient autopilot feature take over and lead me back into the driver's seat of the truck. The keys were still in the ignition where I had left them. I turned them, shifted gears, and maneuvered back into the left turn lane. I got on the freeway and drove home. I couldn't stop thinking about the little bit of blood that leaked from the girl's mouth. Jagged edges of bone piercing her insides. The word *dead*.

I parked the truck perfectly in our driveway. I unlocked the front door and slipped inside, placing the keys in their bowl. I stopped in the bathroom and stared at my face in the mirror. I'd never even contemplated becoming one, but this was the face of a murderer. I shook my head in a silent warning to myself: I could never tell anyone that this happened. The body would be found and it would be chalked up to a hit and run. I hadn't touched or moved her so there would be no evidence. They wouldn't even know what kind of car had hit her. As long as I never told anyone, I wouldn't get caught.

Breaking my usual late-night routine, I turned on the shower and undressed. Halfway through my second shampoo, Dad poked his head into the steamy bathroom. "Robin, you okay?"

"Yeah," I said too emphatically from behind the opaque curtain. "Why?"

"No reason, you just normally don't shower this late."

"I know. Just felt like it. Sorry if I woke you up."

"Oh no, you didn't. I was just kinda dozing, kinda watching TV. Heard you come in but figured you'd go straight to bed."

I made a mental note not to do anything else out of character for the next few weeks. The door squeaked lightly as he started to close it.

"Hey, Dad?" I asked before he left.

"Yeah, Bug?" I smiled as warm water dripped down my face. He hadn't used that nickname for me in a while. My memory flashed to being three or four years old in pajamas with attached feet. Dad would tuck me in and tell me I looked as snug as a bug in a rug.

"I don't feel very good. Might not be able to go to school tomorrow."

"That's okay, I'll write you a note. We have to get this sleep thing under control for you."

He backed out of the bathroom and closed the door so I could finish my shower. When I finally crawled into my own bed, I closed my eyes and half-drifted off. All I could see behind my eyelids were legs at unnatural angles and made-up faces tarnished with blood.

CHAPTER 5

Robin

May 2007

Okay, I admit it. I was in love with Allegra. How could I not be? She was confident, smart, and gorgeous. She made me laugh. She made me feel safe. We'd only known each other for a month, but all I wanted to do was confess my feelings and make her mine for real. The one big snag in this plan was that I still wasn't sure whether or not she actually liked girls.

Since high school graduation a year before, my life had taken on a reliable routine. I woke up late in the morning, worked the afternoon shift at Starbucks, then came home and watched TV while I knitted. On my days off, I cooked vegetable-heavy meals because Dad and I both lived on takeout during work days. I didn't go on late-night drives anymore and was grateful that Dad never asked why. I hadn't bothered to move out and live on my own; there didn't seem to be a point when we had already been living like roommates for years. We usually only saw each other for dinner. He usually tried to go to bed early because, as a construction site manager, he frequently had to be up and moving before dawn. I'm not even sure if he knew that I only slept every third night or so.

Allegra brought much-needed variety into my routine. She waltzed into my life and dusted off every inch of my underutilized spontaneity. Even if we just went out to lunch or a movie, she made it fun. Once she sweet-talked the bartender at Chili's into making her a Long Island Iced Tea, claiming one of her relatives had invented it because her last name was Long.

"That drink was clearly based on the place, Long Island," I'd told her on the drive back to her house.

"I know," she'd replied, "but he believed me and now I've got a buzz, so who's the real winner here?"

"He didn't believe you," I'd exclaimed through laughter. "He just thought you were hot!"

She had just shrugged in response.

One Friday night, Allegra showed up at Starbucks ten minutes before my shift ended. She wore black skinny jeans and a blousy magenta tank top, sandals with a heel, and a long silver chain necklace. Her blonde hair hung in loose waves down her back and around her shoulders. She looked ready for a night out, so it surprised me when her first words to me were, "Tell me this: does your dad keep alcohol in the house?"

I stopped wiping down tables to take her in from head to toe. "Beer, sometimes. What is it with you and drinking all of a sudden?"

"I don't know. I'm graduating in like two weeks. Just feeling antsy. Don't you ever just feel restless no matter what you do? I don't know what will help, but alcohol can't hurt."

"Can't argue with that logic," I replied.

"Beer's gross, though. How do we get something real to drink?"

"I have an idea." I didn't need to explain that I needed to finish wiping down the tables and go clock out. She had come to pick me up at work enough times to know the drill.

In front of the computer in the breakroom, Andre stood staring at the numbers on the clock. He was waiting for them to change to exactly 9:30 so he wouldn't be penalized for clocking out early again. Andre was in his mid-twenties, over six feet tall, and intentionally bald. He was a college graduate in something like English or art history, which made it difficult to find a job in his chosen field. I sometimes heard him grumbling about the lack of professional jobs for someone with his qualifications, but for the most part, he seemed like an okay guy. I had heard through the grapevine of gossipy employees that he had a crush on me, or thought I was cute, or something, but we'd never exchanged more than a greeting.

"Hey, Andre," I said as I hung my green apron on one of the hooks near the door.

"Hey, Robin" he replied in his gruff voice. "How was the last hour?"

"It was fine. Pretty slow. Where were you?"

"They stuck me on drive-thru." He rolled his eyes.

"Ah, that sucks," I commiserated.

An awkward silence penetrated the room. Andre broke it by letting out a sigh of relief and leaning over the keyboard to type in his employee number. "Finally time to go," he said, more to the computer than to me.

"Yay," I cheered lamely. I joined him at the computer and typed in my number when he was finished with his. "Hey, I have a question for you. Feel free to say no."

"What's up?" he asked.

"Well, my friend wants to get drunk, but neither of us is twenty-one. Would you mind…"

"Buying you beer?" He grinned, entertained.

"More like vodka or something. But yeah. Would that be okay?"

"I tell ya what," he said. "If you guys can give me a ride home, we'll stop at the liquor store on the way. Deal?"

I smiled, surprised at how easy that was. "Deal!"

Back in the lobby, I relayed the plan to Allegra. She had borrowed her mom's sedan, so she didn't mind making a couple of short detours on the way to my place. When we finally got there, without Andre but with a large glass bottle of vodka in a paper bag, I realized there was no juice or soda in the house to mix with the liquor.

"Dang, guess we'll have to do shots." I stuck my tongue out disappointedly.

"Have you done shots of this shit before? It cost ten bucks, probably tastes like battery acid," Allegra said.

"It's okay. We can turn it into a game or something. People play drinking games, right?"

"I guess." She grabbed two glasses from a kitchen cabinet and filled them with ice from trays in the freezer.

We walked down the hall. Dad was already snoring loudly in his room. Even though Allegra had been to my house a few times before and seen it messier than it currently was, my cheeks burned when she had to move a pile of clothes off the bed to sit down.

"Should we play Truth or Dare?" I ask.

Allegra groaned. "Ugh, that's so high school."

"Hate to remind you, but you *are* in high school."

"Only for another two weeks! What about Never Have I Ever?"

"Yes, a truly intellectual game and so much better than Truth or Dare." I rolled my eyes.

"Come on, it'll be fun." She had made up her mind, so it was decided. I pulled the bottle out of its paper bag and poured a generous amount into each ice-filled glass.

"Okay, here are the rules. We take turns saying 'never have I ever…' whatever. If you've done the thing, you drink."

"I know."

"Have you played before?"

As much as I wanted to see a glimmer of respect in her eyes, I answered truthfully. "Nope. But I have seen a lot of teen movies."

"Okay, then here's my first one. Never have I ever played Never Have I Ever."

She grinned at her own cleverness, taking a drink from her cup.

"Wait, I thought you only say things you haven't done."

"Well, if you want to drink, you can lie and say something you *have* done," she responded with a grin. "It's still a good way to see if you have shared experiences with the other players."

"Ah, that's a twist I haven't heard before." I gazed into my cup of ice and liquor, trying to think of something I wanted to know about Allegra. "Never have I ever…" My mouth twisted into a private smirk as I thought of the perfect statement. "Never have I ever kissed another girl."

Allegra raised the glass to her lips, hesitated, and then took a sip.

"I knew it!" I hadn't meant to be such a dork about it, but the excitement that she had kissed a girl momentarily took over my body and made me cheer, inside and out.

She had to know exactly what I meant, but she still asked, "Knew what?"

"That you like girls! I knew it! Thought I did, anyway."

"Did your gaydar get all fuzzy when you pointed it at me?"

"Actually, yeah. You're hard to read."

"I try very hard to be hard to read," she said. She took another sip even though she didn't have to, and I realized that I still hadn't touched my own drink. "I'm not... I'm not totally sure that I'm gay, anyway. I've been with guys, too."

"Bet it wasn't as much fun," I said.

She smiled. "It wasn't."

I leaned back against my pillows. "Hey, it's okay to experiment without labels. You're young. There's no harm in taking some time to figure out who you like."

"And what are you, elderly?"

"No, I've just always known I liked girls. Sometimes there's a guy I find cute or something, but they're not..."

"I know what you mean." The understanding in this short sentence was uncharacteristically gentle.

I was grateful that she didn't let me finish the thought. I still wasn't sure exactly what it was that made me fall in love with girls so easily. During high school, I'd had a few boyfriends who faded away almost without me even noticing, and one girlfriend who broke my heart so badly I thought I'd never heal. Beautiful female customers often distracted me to the point of pressing the wrong button on the cash register, but attractive men ordering their drinks with flirty smiles never did. Women just had a way of focusing my attention that men never would.

"So, who was she?" I asked, now incredibly curious about her experience with this other girl.

"Just this dancer chick I met in Phoenix. She doesn't live here."

I wanted to jokingly ask if she was pretending, like the people who claim to be in a long-distance relationship rather than admit they're virgins, but the wistful look in her eyes told me she was being honest.

"Are you guys still...involved, or whatever?"

"Nope. I am free as a bird." Allegra snapped out of her trance and raised her gaze to meet mine. "And it's my turn. Hang on while I think of a good one."

I took my first swig while she thought, and immediately almost spat it out onto the comforter. I had forgotten how rough the first sip of straight liquor was. I sputtered and coughed for a solid minute, and made some dumb joke about the worst being over now. Allegra's tinkling laughter made the burning in my throat worth it.

Two refills and several more Never Have I Ever statements later, the vodka bottle was half-gone and I was splayed diagonally across my bed, drunker than I'd ever been. Allegra seemed sober until she stood up to use the bathroom. She swayed and almost fell back onto the bed twice before actually making it out the bedroom door and down the hall.

I flipped on my small TV for background noise while she was gone. When she came back, she climbed onto the bed and fit herself comfortably into the curves of my body so we were face to face.

"Hi," she said into my collarbone.

"Hey," I said back. I let myself stroke her hair a couple of times before forcing myself to stop. Can't be the creepy older lesbian preying on the mostly straight girl.

"What are we watching?" she asked.

"No idea. Just wanted to put something on so it wasn't so dead silent in here." On the screen, infomercial actors tried an amazing, never-before-seen cleaning product.

"Fair. What time is it?"

I pulled my cell phone out of the pocket of the black work pants I hadn't bothered to change out of. "Almost midnight."

Before I could return my phone to my pocket, Allegra reached up and carefully placed her hand around the back of my neck. Our faces hadn't been that far apart to begin with, but she closed the distance until our noses were a centimeter apart.

"Hi again," she said. I didn't say anything. She kissed me.

The first kiss was soft. A question. Lips on lips for a couple of seconds, then a retreat. She was wordlessly asking if this was okay. To answer, I kissed her back. Her position made it easy for me to cradle her lower back with one arm. I used the other to weave my fingers through her hair and pull her face closer to mine. I was drunk, and she was drunk, but I knew exactly what was happening and I knew she did too.

We fell asleep kissing. The last thing I remember saying was, "You're not going to wake up tomorrow and pretend not to remember this, are you?"

She smiled, eyes closed and teeth pressing into my pillow. "Not a chance."

CHAPTER 6

Robin

October 2007

Allegra graduated high school in May and turned eighteen in August. Getting an apartment together in September fell into place so effortlessly that sometimes I wasn't sure whether it was all a dream. Even after the intimacy of our vodka night, we decided to remain just friends to avoid complicating the new chapter of our lives that was about to begin. This agreement was solidified with the signing of a lease on a two-bedroom apartment in Tempe.

Neither of us had a lot of furniture, so we combed Goodwill until we found a couch and some tables. We both brought our beds from home and put one in each room, but we usually slept together in my room. She said this was because I had a TV in my room and she didn't. We slept in various states of clothing. Sometimes I'd half-wake in the middle of the night and feel her curled around the back of my body, clinging like a koala. The first night she slept in my bed, I got the best rest I had in years. I'd thought this was a fluke or a coincidence, but as soon as Ally started sleeping next to me, I actually started sleeping.

Allegra went to community college a couple of nights a week because her parents paid for it, in addition to giving her a monthly allowance for living expenses contingent on her staying enrolled. She clearly wasn't in the mood to be serious about her studies after only being sprung from high school a few months before, but her parents valued education, and community college placated them for the moment. Allegra frequently speculated that it was only a matter of time before they started bugging her to pick a major and transfer to ASU.

My days at Starbucks stayed the same. I wiped down tables and unpacked boxes of coffee beans. Pissy soccer moms complained that their drink, perfectly made to their specifications, wasn't sweet enough or hot enough. Andre and I commiserated about how obnoxious our manager could be when we were short-staffed. New employees were hired, stayed for a few months, and then moved on. After a while, Andre was the only person left who had been working there when I got hired. Because of this, we formed a united front of senior employees who will not be messed with. Most of the baby seasonal hires thought we were supervisors, and that was fine with us.

One night when Andre and I were clocking out together at nine p.m., he struck up a conversation about Halloween. "This guy I went to school with is having a week-before-Halloween costume party thing tonight," he told me. "He always says he wants his parties to be ragers, but they're usually pretty chill."

"That sounds cool." I didn't really know what response he wanted from me. Was it just information or was this leading to an invite?

"I was thinking about going. Do you want to be my plus one? We can leave if it's lame."

He watched me expectantly. His brown eyes shone under the harsh fluorescent lights embedded in the breakroom ceiling.

"I don't have a costume," I finally exclaimed.

He laughed. It sounded like music. "Me neither. We can go as Starbucks employees."

I smiled. "In that case… Okay. Sure, yeah. Let's go."

"Awesome!"

The party was in a college neighborhood close to ASU. Andre drove, so I texted Allegra on the way there. *I'm going to a Halloween party with Andre. Don't wait up.* After I sent the message, I thought it might sound dismissive. I considered sending another, or at least a smiley face emoticon, but just as quickly decided against it. Per our mutual decision, Allegra was nothing more than my roommate. It didn't matter that I was in love with her. She was still figuring out how she felt about girls in general, let alone me specifically. I couldn't push her into anything she wasn't ready for when she was unsure of her feelings just because I was sure of mine. It wouldn't be fair. I put my phone back in my pocket, and a few minutes later Andre parked against the curb in a cul-de-sac. I was determined to have a good time tonight.

The house was hot and stuffy inside. Too many people breathing and sweating in polyester costumes. In the kitchen, the dining table was covered with at least twenty alcohol bottles. There were mixers as well, so I wouldn't have to relive plain cheap vodka snaking its way down my throat and triggering my gag reflex. Andre seemed to know a lot of the people we passed on the way to the drink table. He poured me something sweet and strong that smelled like coconut and introduced me to several people as "my favorite work friend, Robin." When we had to navigate through a dense group of people, he took my hand and led me through to the other side. His hand was huge, strong, and warm.

After we'd been there for about two hours, I found myself sitting on a couch in the living room between a zombie clown and a sexy nurse. I couldn't remember how many drinks I'd had, but the fuzziness in my brain was rapidly approaching how I'd felt the night Allegra had kissed me. The memory made me smile. "But you're here with Andre tonight," I reminded myself quietly. The people on either side of me didn't seem to notice I was talking to myself. I checked my cell phone. No messages. Oh well.

Andre approached holding two more red plastic cups. He handed one to me and took a long drink from the other.

"Aren't you driving me home?" I asked as I took the cup.

"I am. I switched to Sprite after the first drink."

"Oh." I paused as the information sunk in. "Wait, really?"

"Yeah. I'm a responsible guy. Are you surprised?"

"Kind of? But, no, not really. Sorry. You're nice. Thanks for…being nice."

Andre chuckled. I'm sure my words slurred as I stumbled over the short sentences. He took my hand and pulled me up from the couch. "Ready to go?" he asked.

"Yeah. As soon as I finish this." I chugged from the almost-full cup he had just handed me. "After the first one, you can't actually taste the alcohol at all. That's dangerous," I told him with a grin.

"I know. Welcome to college life."

"Aren't most of your friends graduated?"

"Yeah," he said with a shrug. "But we still drink like college students. I've forgotten everything they tried to teach me about history and geography, but I'll always remember how to drink like a nineteen-year-old."

"Hey, I'm almost nineteen!" I interjected for no reason.

"I always forget how young you are. You're making me feel ancient at twenty-four!" His tone sounded like my age should bother him but he was surprised that it didn't.

He drove me home and parked in the space Allegra and I had been assigned when we moved into the complex even though neither of us owned a car.

"Thanks for bringing me tonight. It was fun." My drunk fingers fumbled as they searched for the door handle.

"It was. We should do it again sometime," Andre said.

"Got another Halloween party invite burning a hole in your Starbucks uniform?"

He laughed. I liked when he laughed at my jokes. "Nah, I think this was the last one except for this total rager I *hate* that always happens on the 31st. I just meant we should have fun again."

"Like a date?" I asked, my jaw slack from drunkenness and surprise.

"Yeah, if that's okay."

"I, um…" I suddenly had no idea what to say. Technically, there was nothing stopping me from saying yes, except that after my last high school boyfriend over two years before, I'd never considered dating a man again. That, and the small matter of my intense and unrequited crush on my unattainable roommate.

I guess I took too long to answer because he started to backtrack his words. "You know what, I'm sorry. Never mind. It's cool if you're not interested. Thanks for coming with me tonight. I'll see you at work."

I put my hand on Andre's arm. "No, that's not it. I'm not *not* interested. I just…" I couldn't think of anything but the truth. "I just haven't thought about dating a man in a really long time."

"Crap. You're gay. I'm so sorry. I didn't mean anything weird, I swear. Just didn't realize."

"I'm not gay, I don't think. Just… Queer? Questioning? I'm one of the Qs in LGBTQ, anyway. Or maybe the B." I paused, waiting for him to respond. He didn't. "But since that's out in the open now, I would like to go out with you again."

Andre's face changed from embarrassed to surprised, eyes widening for a few seconds before he recovered himself into a regular smile. "That's great! I mean, yeah, cool! So…I'll see you at work."

He didn't try to kiss me, which is good because I don't know what I would have done if he had. As I got out of the car, he squeezed my hand the way he had at the party. It was still warm and comforting.

I let myself into our apartment. The bedside lamp was on in my bedroom. I crossed the threshold to see Allegra perched cross-legged on my comforter, eyes glazed with exhaustion, flipping through the TV channels. She wore a pair of my plaid pajama pants and a sports bra. Her hair had been expertly twisted into an intentionally messy bun on top of her head. "Finally," she said as I sat down next to her to take my shoes off. "Why are you still in your work apron?"

"It was my Halloween costume. Didn't you get my message?"

"Yeah," she said. I waited for more, but she didn't say anything else.

I changed into pajamas myself, a tank top and old high school P.E. shorts, and flopped onto the bed next to her.

"Are you okay? You seem pissed or something."

"I'm fine," she replied. Her manner was terse. She hadn't moved since I came into the room.

"Come get comfy, then," I told her. "I'm sure we can find something to watch."

"It's one in the morning, there's nothing but infomercials and reruns from the '70s."

"Well, still…" The buzzing of my cell phone cut me off. I grabbed it from the bedside table where I had put it when I changed out of my work pants. It was a text from Andre: *Thanks again for the fun night. Looking forward to next time!* I smiled like I had a secret, which I guessed I kind of did.

Allegra slid down to the foot of the bed, careful not to brush against me, and stood up. "I'm gonna sleep in my room tonight." Without another word, she left. A few seconds later, I heard her bedroom door close. Even with the leftovers of the strong drinks relaxing my body, I knew sleep wouldn't come until at least dawn without her next to me. I curled up in the warm spot she had left behind and closed my eyes. Bone shards and red-painted lips danced behind my eyelids.

CHAPTER 7

Robin

December 2007

Allegra sat in the corner of our living room couch, curled around a mug of hot coffee. "What do you even know about this dude?"

"What do you mean? Plenty of stuff."

I felt myself gearing up to get defensive because I knew I didn't know much about Andre. We had been dating casually for almost two months. This mostly involved flirting when we worked the same shift and sometimes leaving together to hang out at his apartment because he didn't have any roommates. We made out sometimes, but I was still unsure about having sex with him and he wasn't pressuring. I hated that I was still a virgin, but it felt wrong to lose it to a guy. I kept hoping this would change as I got more comfortable with him.

"Like what?"

"Well… His name is Andre Rivera. He's twenty-four. He works at Starbucks and lives alone. And… He likes pizza and psychological thrillers."

Ally rolled her eyes. "You just described literally every twenty-something guy in existence. No one doesn't like pizza. And you only know his last name because you've seen it on the schedule at work."

I didn't have a response because she was right. Instead of stumbling over more clumsy explanations, I looked around our apartment from my seat next to her on the couch. It was Christmas Eve, but you'd never know it by the state of our place. One thing Ally and I had in common was contempt for temporary decorations. I liked having art hanging on the walls, but only if it could stay up year-round. When we moved in, Ally said she preferred bare walls but didn't care what I hung up as long as I didn't expect her to maintain it. Her bedroom walls were blank and white.

I knew she would see straight through my lame attempt at changing the subject, but I tried anyway. "Why are you drinking coffee at nine at night?"

"It's Christmas Eve. This isn't just coffee, it's Starbucks Christmas Blend. You, of all people, should understand that."

"I mean, it's good, yeah, but the novelty kind of fades away after you pour it every day for two months. Plus Christmas wasn't a huge deal in my house after my mom left 'cause my dad was raised Jewish. We never really did much about Christmas or Hanukkah once it was just the two of us."

"Fair enough." She shrugged and sipped pensively from her steaming mug. "I'll just take some melatonin when it's time to go to sleep. Be gone, caffeine!"

I had been lucky enough to work the morning shift on Christmas Eve and miraculously not be scheduled to work on Christmas Day at all. I was halfway through a bottle of sweet, sticky pink wine Andre had given me as an early present. I drank directly from the bottle and didn't offer to share with Ally. She hadn't mentioned it.

"Hanging out in the living room is stupid," she announced suddenly. "Can we go watch something in your room?"

"Of course." I went in first and turned on the television. Allegra rinsed out her mug in the kitchen sink, then shuffled into her own bedroom where I heard the rattle of her melatonin bottle. When she crossed my threshold I asked, "How many did you take tonight?"

"Just two," she said. "I want to get sleepy, but not be passed out until New Year's."

I channel surfed until landing on a showing of the late-'90s holiday classic, *I'll Be Home for Christmas.*

Allegra literally squealed, a sound I'd never heard from her before. "Oh my god! This was my favorite movie when it came out! I had such a crush on Jonathan Taylor What's-His-Name!"

"Thomas," I said. "I liked it too. Even considering her years of professional-level acting on *7th Heaven*, I think Jessica Biel was at her finest in this movie."

We watched in comfortable silence for a while. The icy demeanor Allegra had greeted me with after the Halloween party had only lasted a few hours. She was back to sleeping in my bed like nothing had happened by November first. In fact, asking me what I knew about him earlier that night was the first time she had mentioned Andre at all since then.

"Hey, Ally?"

"Hmm?"

"Are you mad that I'm dating Andre?"

She opened her eyes and sat up, abandoning the comfortable position she'd found under my blanket. "Not mad necessarily."

"But?" I could tell there was something she wasn't saying.

"But… It's supposed to just be you and me."

"What are you talking about? When we moved in together we agreed to just be friends."

"I only said that because you did," she said, looking down at her hands.

"So… You *did* want to be with me? Like, for real, *with* me?"

She nodded.

This was unbelievable. I had to press the subject. "Did, or do?"

"Did, for sure. Do I still? Like…kind of. But you're dating that stupid dude now."

"Oh jeez." I took a long drink of the wine I'd brought to bed with me.

"What?" She was great at feigning innocence.

"I don't fucking believe this. I pined after you for *months*. You never made a move, and I was too scared to, and then you *agreed with me* that we should just be friends. But *then*, you sleep in my bed every night, half the time in your underwear or less. You can't seriously tell me you don't know that's confusing and hard as hell for me! And then I *finally* started dating someone else, and suddenly *now* you want to be with me? I can't do this back-and-forth thing, Allegra. It's too hard." I huffed and leaned back into the pillows on my side.

"Well, I've been thinking about it a lot more lately. This life we have together… We're already playing house and sleeping together. We care about each other. We share practically everything. And then you stop spending as much time here because you're off with this dumb guy… I got jealous."

"You got jealous," I repeat monosyllabically.

"Yeah, what—"

"Nothing, I'm just trying to fucking process this."

We sat in silence for several minutes. On the screen, JTT charmingly invited Jessica Biel for a ride in Santa's sleigh. Jessica forgave all his lies and climbed right in, because this was a holiday rom-com and there could be no other ending.

Finally, Allegra spoke again. "I didn't think I'd want to be with you like that. I thought that night we kissed was a fluke, and it just meant we had a deep connection as friends or something. But since you've been dating *him*, I've started thinking about how it could be if you were dating me instead. I get jealous when you leave to hang out with him. I want to hide in the backseat of his car and strangle him from behind."

"That is oddly specific," I said, taking another drink from the wine bottle.

"Never have I ever fantasized about killing your boyfriend." She plucked the bottle out of my hand and brought it to her own mouth. She took a long drink of wine and then fixed me with intense eye contact to emphasize her point.

"That's not funny," I tell her.

"Wasn't meant to be," she retorts.

"What are you even talking about?"

"I like to think about killing people," she said as if she was telling me her favorite color was pink. "Imagine causing them pain. Watching their faces. Hearing them scream."

"You wouldn't if you'd actually hurt someone like that," I muttered quietly, forgetting she was still close enough to hear me.

Allegra smiled like a little kid with a delicious secret she was eager to share. "Yes, I would. I used to catch squirrels and torture them in my backyard. Their little screams and the way they fought and bled always made me wonder what it would be like to do that to a person."

"That's a little creepy, Ally. But a lot of kids do weird shit like that and then grow up to be perfectly normal."

"I did it until I moved out of my parents' house." She didn't look concerned or ashamed. It was just a hobby to her. She might as well have been telling me about promoting to a new belt color in karate.

The next second, she blew off the subject easily in favor of an even more uncomfortable one. "Anyway," she said, "what did you mean about not wanting to think about hurting someone if I'd actually done it?"

Shit, I thought. I'd really thought she would let that comment go, which was dumb on my part, honestly. "Just that…it's probably a lot harder emotionally than you think it would be."

"No. You sounded like you knew."

Sometimes I could swear she could see exactly what was going on inside my head.

"Have you hurt someone?" She asked quietly, trying not to scare away this delicate moment of opportunity. "What haven't you told me?"

Fuck. I wracked my brain in the precious seconds I had to make up a lie and came up with nothing. If I clammed up, she'd never let it go. There was no other choice. "I… Yeah. But it was a while ago. I was just trying to tell you that it doesn't feel good."

Ally's body language changed completely. If she'd had a chair, she would have slid her perfect ass to the very edge of it. "Tell me everything. How did you do it? *Why* did you do it? Did they piss you off? They died, right? I feel like you wouldn't be taking this so seriously unless they died."

"I really don't want to talk about this." The subject felt macabre against the backdrop of Christmas Eve.

"Well, now you have to," she mandated.

I shook my head and drank more wine. I was climbing up to a pretty high buzz, but it was tainted by memories of the girl with the broken leg and internal injuries, a thin line of blood spilling from her lips. I closed my eyes and shook my head again, trying to dislodge the images from my brain.

When I opened my eyes, Allegra had inched closer to me. She put her hand on the back of my neck and kissed me, and holy shit that single kiss was better than all the time I'd spent with Andre combined. She kissed me, and I felt it everywhere in my body at once and my mind was empty of anything except her mouth and her smell and the feeling of my fingers tangled in her soft hair.

She pulled away and whispered, "Please tell me."

She left me breathless. I was literally panting. I knew she was using my feelings for her as a way to get the information she thought she needed. At least, that's what it felt like. It was also possible that she really did have feelings for me and had chosen the wrong moment to express them. As soon as I could take a deep breath, I used it to tell her about the accident.

"And you didn't call the cops?" She asked when I thought I'd given enough detail.

"No. I was afraid I'd get in trouble. The longer I waited, the more I thought they'd nail me for murder instead of the other one. Manslaughter, I think, right?"

"Manslaughter… Man's laughter… That's how I remember how to spell it. You're right, though, that is the lesser charge. What did her face look like? Her eyes?"

"She was wearing a lot of makeup. Her eyeliner and lipstick were perfect. None of it even got smudged. That's what I see when I close my eyes but can't sleep: Her perfect lipstick staying in place even as the blood drips from her mouth."

"Blood came out of her *mouth*?" She was so excited. I'd never considered being excited about blood.

"Yeah. I think maybe her ribs broke and caused internal bleeding or something."

"What about her eyes though?" Ally's own eyes were shining with morbid enthusiasm in the TV's glow. She wasn't even trying to hide it.

"They were brown. And big. And she looked scared. She stared at me almost the whole time I sat there. But she couldn't talk. Or maybe she could and just didn't."

"Did you watch the life leave them?"

"Yeah. It was the most terrifying thing that's ever happened to me. But it also felt weirdly powerful? Like, she lost her life, and I did it. I took it from her. I hate myself for thinking that, but I never thought I had the power to do something so…permanent. Even though, technically, my dad's car did it. But I was controlling it. You know what I mean. God. I'm such a heinous person. Can't believe I didn't call the cops and just confess."

"Holy shit," Ally whispered. "You just sat there on the curb and watched."

"Yeah. I was in shock. I watched her die and then I just…left."

"You sat there and watched her die. And then just left and went on with your life." She spoke slowly, mostly to herself, processing my terrible story.

"I've never told anyone this before," I said, suddenly panicking. "You can't say a word about it."

Allegra drew an X on her chest with her index finger, a silent way of saying *cross my heart and hope to die.*

Several minutes went by, and she just sat quietly, looking at me. Finally I said, "What?"

"Nothing. I just… I want what you have."

"What, guilt and PTSD from watching someone literally die at my hands?"

She smiled broadly. "You have the heart of a killer."

I was horrified. "Jesus. I hope not."

"Hey, hey. It's not a bad thing," she comforted. "I wish I'd had an experience like that. I wish I could have killed someone by accident first. Popped my murder cherry early." She stuck out her tongue playfully as if we were joking about school or our love lives.

I didn't know what to do now that I'd actually told another person my darkest secret. I leaned back against my pillows and drank more wine. The bottle was almost empty by now. I passed it to Ally and she drained the dregs, then set it on the floor next to the bed and scooted closer to me to lay her head on my chest. It felt almost normal. It could have been any other night in our apartment, in my bed, not necessarily one where we'd both just made first-time confessions. I stroked her hair a few times. Her breathing became heavier and more even. She wasn't asleep yet, but I could tell she was getting there.

"Robin," she said softly.

"Yeah?"

"We should kill someone together. I've always wanted to, and you already know how. We're perfect for each other."

I didn't answer because it felt like such a ridiculous request. I wanted to stay like this forever, with Ally snuggled against me in our cozy bed. She had mildly freaked me out with all the murder talk, but that didn't make me love her any less. Like the short shelf life of her anger about my dates with Andre, I was sure my surprise would wear off by morning. I closed my eyes and breathed in the smell of her strawberry conditioner. When I was sure she was asleep, my body started to relax. My eyelids drooped and eventually closed on their own.

"Robin," Allegra whispered again.

"What?"

"We're gonna do it, right?"

I didn't want to answer, but just as sure as I knew that I would soon be breaking up with the safe, unassuming straight boy I was trying to convince myself to love, I knew that Ally and I would kill someone together. She had made up her mind, so it was decided.

CHAPTER 8

Robin

December 2007

In my defense, I'd never broken up with anyone before. My brief flirtations in high school couldn't really be considered relationships, especially since they had all dissolved on their own with minimal drama. The one notable exception was the girlfriend who broke my heart, and *she* broke up with *me* while I begged her not to. Twice.

Allegra had coached me on how to break up with Andre that morning, but as I donned my green apron and clocked in for my afternoon shift, I knew I wasn't prepared. Andre caught my eye from his post at the drive-thru station. I smiled sympathetically as I passed on my way to the front counter. From obnoxiously loud orderers to people who held up the line by swearing they ordered seven pumps and it tasted like six, no one liked drive-thru duty. *Great, he'll be in a shitty mood to begin with,* I thought as I used my employee ID number to unlock the cash register.

Miraculously, the indoor line was empty and there were hardly any customers sitting in the cafe. It looked like it would be a slow afternoon until people started leaving work and school and swinging by our shop for some caffeine to keep them going until bedtime. I inhaled the mixed aromas of freshly ground coffee beans, hot liquid sugar, and dusty desert air swirling inside when someone entered through the swinging glass door.

I felt the warm pressure of a hand on each of my hips, then a quick kiss just below my left ear. "Hey, Babe," Andre said softly from behind me.

I screwed an everything-is-fine smile firmly into place before turning around.

"Hi," I answered, letting his hands stay put as I spun to look at him. "I saw you got stuck at the window again… Sorry."

He shrugged. "No big deal. I only have to stay there 'til Jenn comes in at four. Hey, what time are you off today? Want to grab dinner or something after work?"

I shook my head, pressing my lips together in a thin line. "Not tonight. Sorry."

"Ah, no worries. Let's at least take our break together though, okay?"

I nodded before it dawned on me that I was leading Andre on after I'd already decided to dump him. Agreeing to hang out with him on break was basically just me pretending everything was fine between us because I was too chicken to tell him we were done. Then again, I was also providing myself with an opportunity to talk to him alone.

"Okay, I have to get back. Just wanted to say hi." He shot me a sweet grin and sauntered back to the drive-thru window, adjusting his headset as he went.

Just as I'd guessed, the store got busy about an hour after I got there. I didn't have much time to think about my impending talk with Andre as I struggled to hear people's names and orders over the buzz of voices in the lobby and machines behind the counter. Jenn, a senior at ASU with a surly demeanor and the longest blonde hair I'd ever seen, tapped me on the shoulder just after four.

"Brian sent me to take your spot so you can have your break. Then he wants you to go unpack the new merch shipment with Andre."

"Why? He never puts Andre and me together on stuff."

She rolled her eyes. "I don't know, I just know I'm supposed to work your register."

"Right, sorry." I signed off and stepped away so Jenn could take my place. I slunk off to the break room, not looking forward to spending the entire evening working alongside my soon-to-be-ex boyfriend.

I sat at the gray plastic table and stared at my hands. A few minutes passed in deafening silence before Andre entered. He tossed something into my lap before claiming the seat next to me. The object's package crinkled as I moved to pick it up. When I saw that he'd brought me dark chocolate–covered graham crackers, my favorite food item offered by Starbucks, I almost chickened out. I considered staying with him forever out of sheer awkwardness. We'd get married and have little closeted babies whose mother has been carrying on a secret affair with Auntie Allegra since before they were born. He was kinda dumb. It could work.

But then, I considered the outcome of breaking up with him. An afternoon of discomfort and some weird eye contact in exchange for being Allegra's actual girlfriend. She had used that word specifically. Girlfriend. She wanted to be my girlfriend. She wanted *me*. I didn't know how to do my makeup, and I felt more comfortable in a one-piece bathing suit than a bikini, and my shoulder-length hair sometimes frizzed at odd angles, and I was a virgin, and I told people I was bi even though I secretly knew I didn't really have feelings for men, which actually made me a self-hating, closeted lesbian who'd never even seen any boobs besides my own before moving in with Allegra, and I was too scared to refer to myself as a lesbian out loud for fear it would really be true, and still. Still, she wanted me. I had to do this.

"Andre." My instinct was to ask his name like a question, but I adjusted the last syllable of his name as it left my mouth so it came out as a semi-strong statement.

"Yeah, Babe?"

I groaned internally. I hated that fucking nickname. It sounded juvenile and controlling all at once. Like I was his child, but also his property.

"Okay, so—"

"Oh, before I forget," he interrupted, "my friend from college is in this acoustic indie band, something about three guitars and no drums, I dunno. Anyway, they're playing at a little independent coffee shop in Scottsdale this weekend. I thought it might be fun to go together."

"Um…maybe…"

"I mean, I know we're both around coffee too much as it is, but it'd be a fun date." He shrugged and waited for me to answer.

"I, um, can't."

"Okay…" He trailed off, confusion showing on his furrowed forehead. He wasn't used to me saying no to hanging out without an excuse. I could have claimed to be going sky diving this weekend for all he cared; he never checked up on the reasons I claimed I couldn't see him. He was remarkably understanding about my too-close friendship with Allegra. I even thought he might have known my feelings for her were stronger than I admitted. He had never even been interested in meeting her after the one night he'd bought vodka for us in exchange for a ride home. He seemed immune to the charisma that made all other guys fall at her feet. If I were straight, he would have been perfect for me.

I fiddled with the package of graham crackers for a few seconds, silent except for the sound of the plastic wrapper, before sliding them across the gray table. He picked them up when they were within his reach and looked at me quizzically. "Did I get the wrong ones? I thought it was dark chocolate that you liked, but I can switch it for milk chocolate if you want."

"No, I— Dark chocolate's great. I just can't…take them."

"Why not?"

Oh my god, just take the hint! I knew giving back a single snack wasn't enough to imply a breakup, but my brain was screaming to be finished with this conversation.

"Just not hungry." I shrugged and smiled without teeth.

"Oh. Okay."

My uneasiness grew the longer we sat in silence. Finally, I decided to say something that I couldn't go back on, even if I chickened out halfway through. This was my trick for having difficult conversations: say something that's easier than the news you have to give, but something that you can't cover up with pleasantries. For example, saying *I need to talk to you about something important* provides no obvious path out of the conversation except to tell them something important. You can't even beg off with a shallow excuse that's obviously a lie, because whatever you come up with probably won't be important enough for the grave tone you started the conversation with. I groaned internally, took a deep breath, and braced my palms against the plastic table.

"There's another reason I don't want the graham crackers but…" I'd started strong but the rest of the sentence had somehow gotten lost in my mounting anxiety.

"Um, okay…" Andre waited for me to continue, but I didn't. "What is it?" he prompted.

"I don't think we should, um, hang out anymore."

My face twisted into a distorted grimace as I waited for his answer, but I couldn't help it. When I opened my eyes, Andre looked surprisingly calm. His lips were pressed together and he sort of nodded like he wasn't surprised.

"I kinda saw this coming," he said quietly.

"What do you mean?"

"Well, I figured you were either just really inexperienced and timid, or you just weren't into me."

Little do you know, it's both! I figured this wasn't a joke that I should make aloud at this particular moment. "Yeah… I'm sorry, Andre."

"Hey, don't be sorry. You can't help it if you're not into it." He shrugged.

"It's not that I'm not into it. I just…"

"Don't worry about it, Babe."

I winced.

"Guess I shouldn't call you that anymore, huh?"

"Guess not," I said with relief. Honestly, losing the grating nickname was probably the best thing that would come out of the breakup.

I was so relieved that he didn't get upset or violent. Andre had never shown me a violent side and had always seemed like a very level-headed guy, but there were too many stories of rejected guys snapping to ever put me completely at ease in this type of situation.

I smiled genuinely at Andre. "I really am sorry. And it's nothing about you. It's my own shit, I swear."

"Ah, 'It's not you, it's me.' Oldest line in the book." He smiled to show he was joking. That smile made me wonder if I was making the right decision. Where would I ever find a man as understanding as him again? I dismissed the internal question as soon as it occurred. Beginning to accept that I was, in fact, not romantically interested in men also came with the unexpected task of reforming my subconscious thoughts to remind myself that heteronormativity wasn't the only path I was allowed to see for my future.

"No, I swear, it really *is* me. I'm, um…"

"Gay?"

My eyes widened in fear of having been identified before I'd even fully accepted the fact myself. Was it that obvious?

"Don't worry, I won't out you to anyone. I wasn't even completely sure until you just looked at me like that."

"Like what?" I asked, trying to rearrange my face into a less incriminating expression.

"Like I just told everyone in fifth grade that you still sleep with a teddy bear."

"I might actually just be bi," I mumbled. "Maybe after I figure some stuff out, you and I can…"

"Is that really what you want?"

"No." The single word was quieter than my mumbling had been, but he still heard and nodded.

"Hey, shit happens." Andre stood up and clapped one hand gently down on my shoulder. "It's all good. We're good. Don't worry about it."

"And we can still be friends?"

"Of course. I don't hate you just because we didn't work out."

"I'm honestly shocked about that," I told him, turning to look up at his face.

"Yeah, some guys are jerks. That's just not worth it to me, you know? I'd rather be friends, or whatever, than sit around planning revenge."

I didn't know what to say to that, so I stayed quiet. After a few seconds, our still vignette of Awkward Lesbian and Understanding Ex-Boyfriend was ruined by routine human movements. Andre took his hand off my shoulder and moved toward the breakroom door, unwrapping the graham crackers as he went.

"I think I'm gonna take the rest of the day off," he said. "I have some sick time I can use. Kinda just feel like vegging out at home."

"Darn, I guess Brian'll have to find me another partner to unpack freight with all night." I hadn't been sure about trying a joke, but Andre rewarded my effort with a genuine chuckle.

"Sounds like fun. I'll see you later, Robin." He left the room, probably off to find Brian and fake some mild illness that would get him out of work for the afternoon but believably let him come back tomorrow without any reduced paychecks.

As soon as Andre was out of the room, I let out a huge breath I hadn't realized I had been holding. How had I even been able to carry on a conversation with that much extra air in my lungs?

I was also incredulous for a different reason: I'd done it! I broke up with my first, and possibly last, actual boyfriend without any bloodshed whatsoever.

Even though I felt bad for breaking up with Andre, I veritably floated through the remaining four hours of my shift. Of course, I texted Allegra to let her know I'd done the deed, but I couldn't wait to get home and tell her in person how much of a non-issue it was. I was delighted by my ability to break bad news to someone and have them take it well, although that might have been more about his understanding nature than my tripping around cliché breakup phrases like "It's not you, it's me." I was also delighted that unpacking merch freight with Jenn that afternoon wasn't nearly as obnoxious as I'd anticipated. We actually talked like two humans even though she and her fellow cheerleaders would have shoved my head down the toilet in high school, and her insanely long hair only got caught in a zip tie one time. Most of all, I was delighted by the possibility of my relationship with Allegra blossoming now that there was nothing in our way.

I'd forgotten all about Ally asking me, when she was half-asleep and I was a little more than half-drunk, if we could kill someone together. I was sure it was just one of those weird, loopy late-night questions that would never come of anything concrete. That afternoon, I only knew that I would be coming home to my girlfriend.

PART TWO

CHAPTER 9

Allegra

January 2008

My cell phone lit up the dark room, practically buzzing off Robin's night-stand as someone called from a blocked number. I had no idea what time it was, but a small amount of sunlight streamed through gaps in the window blinds. I grabbed the phone and flipped it open.

"Hello?"

"Hi, Allegra? It's Andrea from the dance team! How are you?"

"Andrea, hi." I cleared my throat and sat up in bed. "I'm okay, how are you doing?"

"Good, good!"

It had been eight months since high school graduation. I'd received my final grades and diploma, and I'd returned all my library books and dance team uniform pieces like I was supposed to. What could Andrea possibly want? I didn't prompt her to speak again, just waited for her to continue while I rubbed my eyes and tried to wake up a little. Robin stirred next to me but didn't wake up.

"So, listen, Allegra. We're working on pieces for the end-of-the-year performance, and I was wondering if you'd like to come back and set a piece on the group."

"Like, choreograph?"

"Yes! The theme for our part of the recital this year is all alumni-created pieces. I thought of you first because you always had such original ideas."

"Um… How many pieces will the dance team have in the show this year?" The dance studio closest to our school, Powerhouse Dance, lets our varsity team perform a few numbers in their June recital every year in exchange for us letting them use our large school theater for the show. Our contributions were usually just extra-practiced versions of whatever we'd performed at pep rallies, and I knew the purpose was to advertise our high school dance program to the parents of younger dancers, but it was still nice to feel like working all year on routines and technique had an end goal besides attempting to get our fellow students excited about subpar sports teams.

"Powerhouse had fewer numbers than usual this year, so they're giving us five to make their show longer. I was hoping you'd like to do one, maybe Kaitlin or Karen would come back to set one, and the rest will go to some other alumni."

"Hmm." I glanced at Robin, who was slowly starting to wake up. She squinted at me and pointed at the phone, wondering who I was talking to. I held up a finger and smiled, conveying that I'd tell her everything after I hung up.

"So, what do you think? Are you in?"

"I, ah… When would you need me? And how often?"

"Oh man," Andrea chirped, "I'm so ahead of myself! Of course you need the logistics. Well, dance team still meets at the same time, 3:30 to 5:00 on Monday, Wednesday, and Friday. I figure I'll give each choreographer an hour of practice every week, which also leaves some time for me to teach a little bit." She laughed at her own weak joke. I'd forgotten how unbearably upbeat she was. "You're the first person I've called, so you can have your choice of timeslots! I don't know if you're in college, or working, or anything, but do any of those days work better for you than others?"

"Andrea, can you hang on for just a second?"

"Oh yeah, sure, no problem!"

I covered the phone's speaker and turned to face Robin, who was now propped against the headboard combing clawed fingers through her hair in an attempt to get it out of her face. I was always telling her to put it in a ponytail before bed, but most of the time she drifted off unexpectedly. This resulted in almost every strand of her light brown, shoulder-length hair being somehow both tangled and stuck to her face by morning.

"It's Andrea from dance team," I told her quietly.

"The teacher? What does she want?"

"She wants me to set a piece on the team for the June show. I'd have to go in weekly until then to teach it and have them practice it and all. Should I do it?"

"Hmm…" She thought it over, wrinkles appearing on her forehead for just a few seconds. "Do you *want* to? Will you have time to come up with a piece and everything, with school?"

"Come on, you know school's a joke."

Robin shrugged. "Then, I don't see why not."

I put the phone back to my ear. "Andrea?"

"I'm still here!"

"Good. Well, I'll do a piece for the concert, sure."

Andrea literally squealed into the phone. "That's so great! I'm sure you'll do a great job. This is your cell phone number, right? Is it okay if I send you a text later with more details?"

"Yeah, that's fine," I told her.

"Oh, and did you already tell me which day of the week you wanted?"

"No. How 'bout Mondays?"

"Sounds great. I'll see you soon!"

"Okay, Andrea. Bye." I flipped my phone shut and flopped dramatically against the pillows. "Why did I just agree to that?" I asked Robin.

"Um, because you have nothing better to do?" She grinned, then leaned over and kissed my forehead with a loud smack.

"Oh yeah, you're right." I looked at my phone again to find out how late in the morning and/or early in the afternoon we'd slept today. It was 11:20 a.m., which was pretty respectable considering we hadn't gone to bed before three that morning. Robin's Starbucks shifts never started before the early afternoon, and I only signed up for afternoon and evening classes on purpose, so over the last couple of months, we had modified our sleep schedule to be somewhere between a night-shift worker's and an exotic dancer's. I couldn't remember the last time I'd woken up before ten a.m. The more I stayed up all night, the more I hated daylight.

I knew Robin had always been a night owl. She'd had insomnia as a teenager and used to drive around until she got tired, but after killing that girl, she had turned her preexisting love for knitting into a safer insomniac hobby. The first few months we were roommates, I'd wake up in the middle of the night to use the bathroom and be surprised to find her in the living room with all the lights on, knitting a hat and listening to emo music loudly in her headphones. I'd thought crafty people were messy with their supplies, but there had been no clues left around the apartment that she was a knitting fiend until I walked in on her wild middle-of-the-night yarn party. She didn't even seem to keep extra yarn around, preferring to buy exactly what she needed for a project and toss or donate the excess when it was finished.

After I discovered it by accident, Robin wasn't so secretive about her knitting. She'd sometimes even work on a blanket or a scarf when we watched movies together. After she broke up with Andre, Robin finally admitted that she was embarrassed by the hobby because it seemed "old ladyish," but it helped distract her brain for a while so she could be involved with whatever was happening in the moment, and I couldn't see anything wrong with that.

I swung my legs over the side of the bed, yawned again, and rotated my ankles and wrists to begin waking up my body. Robin rolled over and squinted at me from underneath the curtain of her hair.

"Why are you getting up so early?" she asked groggily. "Come back and cuddle."

"I want coffee. The phone woke me up, and now I'm awake for the day."

"Hmm." Her eyes drifted shut again.

I left the bedroom, closing the door behind me, and made my way to the kitchen. While filling up the coffee pot, I considered what song I should use for my dance team piece and how I should dress the dancers. The only song that came to mind was "I Kissed a Girl" by Katy Perry because it had been on the radio nonstop lately. It was a good song, but already so overplayed that I couldn't imagine listening to it on repeat for the next four months while simultaneously teaching a group of high schoolers.

As the coffee started to drip and the pot started to steam up, Robin wandered into the kitchen. Her hair was still a mess, and she looked adorable in her oversized sleep shirt and cotton underwear. I held my arm out, and she gravitated toward me, laying her head on my shoulder. After a few seconds, I felt her temple move as she opened her mouth in a yawn.

"So, guess what," I said.

She shook her head, gently moving my shoulder with it. "It's too early to guess what."

"Guess anyway."

"Um… You won the lottery and were just waiting for the right time to tell me that I can quit Starbucks and open the Etsy shop of my dreams?"

I laughed. "I wish. Almost as good. I came up with a plan!"

"A plan for what? How you're gonna juggle school, doing that Andrea thing, and maintain a relationship with your super cute and awesome girlfriend?"

"Well, of course I'll be doing that," I smirked sideways at her. "But I already told you school's a joke. I might even take a semester off, who cares. A plan for…you know."

Robin took her head off my shoulder so she could look at my face. I guess I should have known better than to start this conversation before caffeine, but I'd been thinking about it for a few days and really couldn't see too many downsides. I smiled to let her know it was a positive announcement.

"I thought of a plan for how we can kill someone and get away with it." My smile grew until I was beaming.

"Oh, holy shit, you were serious about that?" Robin stepped a few inches away from me and busied herself at the cabinet, looking for mugs and spoons.

"Of course I was. I thought I told you how important this was to me."

"Ally, it's not like you're asking my opinion about a car you want to buy. You're telling me you want to *kill* someone. Not only that, you want me to help! Like…no!"

"'Like no?' That's your only argument?"

"Because I shouldn't have to come up with an argument for why we're not gonna kill someone! At the very least, I've already done it once and gotten away with it. I'm not great at math, but I'm good enough to know that, in itself, is a statistical miracle. The odds I'd get away with it again are probably negative seventeen thousand percent!"

I came up behind Robin, encircled her waist with my arms, and kissed the back of her neck. "Can I at least tell you the plan?" I asked with my chin on her shoulder. "It's really good."

She sighed and turned around to face me, staying inside my embrace. "Fine. What is the plan?"

I did a jaunty little dance on my way back to the coffee pot. Robin handed me two mugs, and I poured coffee into both, then handed them back so she could add sugar and cream. While we performed this familiar exchange, I told her the plan.

"Okay. I've been thinking about this for over a week and it's pretty foolproof. So, you know how my mom runs that homeless shelter out in Cave Creek? It's far from here, and we don't know anyone out there, so, no connections. I say we go down there and lure one of the kids from the shelter to come home with us."

Robin stirred her coffee pensively. "I don't really want to *lure* anyone anywhere," she said to her mug's swirling contents.

"So we lure him here, and have all the stuff set up already in the second bedroom."

"*Your* bedroom?"

"Um…yeah. Anyway. We have everything set up in the second bedroom, and we tie him up and kill him, and then break down the body in the bathtub like they do on TV!"

The main part of the scenario relayed, I took a noisy slurp of my coffee. Robin didn't say anything, so I prompted her with a nudge. "What do you think?"

She shrugged. "I guess I just don't want to be involved in anyone else dying."

"Come on!" I skipped over to the spare bedroom door, opened it, and gestured inside dramatically. "Wouldn't this make the perfect kill area?"

Robin joined me in the doorway and peered inside. The bed was perfectly made and absolutely nothing hung on the walls. Similar to my bedroom at my parents' house, I kept this room tidy and plain. She probably hadn't even seen this room in weeks. We never used it. I only visited daily to get clothes out of my dresser.

"Why don't you just think about my genius plan for a few days? I know you'll come around to it. How could you not?"

"How could I not…" Her words faded away as she retreated back to her/our bedroom. I heard the TV switch on and some daytime talk show audience applauded as I crossed the apartment to curl up on the living room couch with my coffee.

Chapter 10

Robin

January 2008

Allegra brought up the murder thing again completely out of the blue. I wasn't expecting to be asked if I thought murdering a homeless teenager was a great idea ten minutes after I woke up. I especially wasn't expecting her to have a fully thought-out plan that she expected me to agree with immediately. It had taken me however many months to admit I didn't want to be with Andre, and that was something I *wanted* to do. She should have known I'd need some time to think.

I was in my room alone for a change, listening to music on my phone without headphones because Ally was having her coffee in the living room. Sometimes, when we were in the apartment together but not in the same room, I felt like she used geography against me. The vibe in the apartment went from casual to toxic in a matter of minutes as she pouted and sighed just outside of my line of sight. She expected me to come out there and tell her that her plan was brilliant, she was brilliant, and I was on board, no questions asked. This was the first time I wasn't willing to give her exactly what she wanted, exactly when she wanted it.

I went to my closet and examined the small yarn stash that I kept in a reusable shopping bag hanging next to my sweaters. I wanted to start a new project, maybe something for Ally since I hadn't knitted her anything yet. My eyes were immediately drawn to a skein of soft lilac with little flecks of tan. The label pictured a peaceful woman in a cowboy hat, and I could definitely see how spinning it into certain overlace patterns would be reminiscent of burlap, cocktails in canning jars, and shouting "yee haw!"

I picked up the skein and considered what size needles I'd need to use with it, but second-guessed myself and returned it to the bag. Neither the color nor the country vibe were right for Allegra.

I reached deep into the bag and blindly grabbed a skein that felt feathery soft like a down comforter. When I brought the yarn into the light, I examined the light gray strand accented with a few thin pieces of silver thread running down the sides. It appeared to be in good shape even though the label had been lost somewhere, and the subtly glamorous vibe would definitely match Ally's usual aesthetic.

I chose a pair of needles and bobbed my head to whatever Regina Spektor–like song the Pandora website had chosen for me as I considered how wide of a scarf she might like. Would she even like me to make her something at all, or was it too soon for random acts of gifting? We had been together for three weeks and a couple of days. Together, as in solidly identifying as a couple. Allegra was my girlfriend. We still slept in the same bed every night, only now we kissed goodnight. We had made out exactly four times, allowing our hands to explore a little further underneath waistbands and hems in each session.

She hadn't pressured me to have sex exactly, but I knew that she wanted to. Allegra had slept with a lot of guys, in addition to making out with at least one other girl, and I was intimidated, either by her experience or my lack thereof. I was still trying to make sure I did the girlfriend part right; sex was another animal completely. Maybe a perfect slip-stitched scarf would say what my mouth couldn't: "The reason we haven't had sex yet has nothing to do with you, I'm just terrified that I'll be bad at it. I like you more than anyone else I've dated, and that's probably why I'm even more nervous to take that step with you." Unfortunately, until I could stop being an incredibly awkward, shy, gay-ass goblin, I'd have to replace seduction with heartfelt gifts. I started the first few rows of the scarf, biting my lip until it tasted sour.

As I drank my coffee, I momentarily toyed with the possibility that she had switched desires from sex to murder, and as long as I helped with the murder, I wouldn't have to worry about sex until I was ready. I doubted that though. On my TV, Maury Povich told someone they were not the father. I settled into the pillows and quieted my racing thoughts with the rhythmic click of my needles.

During my second episode of Maury, Allegra came into the room looking sheepish. That expression was the closest she ever got to apologizing, so I wordlessly accepted. She crossed to the bed and sat down next to me.

"Whatcha doin'?" she asked.

"Same thing I'm always doing," I answered, slightly harsher than I meant to. If she noticed my biting tone, she didn't acknowledge it.

She picked up the small completed section of scarf and rubbed it on her cheek. "This yarn is so soft."

"I'm glad you like it. It's for you." So much for keeping the secret.

"Seriously? Cool!" Ally exclaimed. She didn't ask why.

—

I got home from work around midnight. My hair had frizzed halfway out of its ponytail, and my purse was heavy on my shoulder. As soon as I stepped into the apartment, I smelled coffee, which must have meant Allegra was up late waiting for me. Sure enough, she was in my room watching TV and idly flipping through some magazine that had come in the mail earlier that week. When she sipped from her mug, her curtain of blonde hair fell forward and obscured her face. Sometimes it felt like coffee was an entire food group in our house.

"How was work?" she asked as I dropped my purse on the floor.

"I got stuck on the drive-thru for, like, five hours," I told her with an exasperated sigh.

She made a grossed-out face, knowing this was the worst position in the store. "At least you're off tomorrow, right?"

"Yeah, that's the good part. I'm gonna take a shower." I grabbed a towel and made my way to the bathroom.

I didn't undress until I was in the bathroom with the door closed, even though Ally had seen me in my underwear before. I was too tired to think about looking good naked. I turned on the water and waited for it to warm up, checking the temperature with my hand every few seconds. When it was properly scalding, I stepped in and let the stream wash away all the spilled milk and entitled customers.

While massaging shampoo into my scalp, I heard the bathroom door open. I poked my head out from behind the curtain and saw Allegra, wearing only a pair of underwear, standing in front of the shower.

"Mind if I join you?" she asked, tugging at her underwear until it dropped, pooling around her ankles. Her hair hung long and straight, almost covering her nipples but not quite. God, she was stunning. I didn't know what to say, so I just nodded.

She climbed into the shower, and we stood facing each other, seeing one another fully for the first time. I kissed her just to ground myself in the moment. Could I possibly be so lucky? When she returned my kiss and took it one step farther by finding my tongue with her own, I knew it was real.

We started making out furiously, open mouths connected and tongues searching hungrily. Her hair had turned to thick ropes almost immediately in the spray of warm water, and I moved one of them off her shoulder so I could explore her neck and chest with my mouth. I don't know how I knew how to do this, but it came naturally and felt so good. As I licked and nibbled at her neck, Allegra actually let out a small moan.

She grabbed my shoulders and gently turned me around so my back was to her. I braced myself on the wall of the shower as she explored my body with her hands. Every touch was one I wished would last forever. Finally, she made her way south of my waist. I wasn't timid anymore. It felt perfect. I let her tease me with her soft fingers and tongue from behind until the tightening in my abdomen exploded into an orgasm. My knees went so weak that I almost fell to the floor of the shower, but she held me up until I regained my strength.

Panting, I said, "I love you."

Ally helped me rinse my hair, still slick with forgotten shampoo. I turned off the water and we both stepped out of the tub. We went to my bedroom in towels and laid our wet heads on the pillows.

It wasn't long before I was unwrapping the gift of her bare, glistening skin. We kissed again, my greedy hands roaming every inch of her. I tasted the delicate skin of her neck, shoulders, breasts, nipples, and stomach, each a little different. I lapped up the leftover water droplets from her inner thighs, which made her gasp and moan. I couldn't believe how easy this all was. I had just been stressing out about our first time earlier that day, and now here it was, effortless.

"Is the first time always like that?" I asked later, when the urgency was over and we had finally caught our breath.

"God, no. My first time could hardly even be considered sex." She rolled her eyes.

"Well, you know my first-time story. You were there. Can I hear yours?"

"There's not much to tell. I was about twelve, the guy was probably about seventeen or eighteen. I seduced him just to see if I could. Turns out, not even the threat of arrest can keep men away from a tight little underage pussy."

"You mean, he knew how old you were?"

"Of course. It was part of the challenge."

"For him, or for you?"

She didn't respond with anything more than a shrug, so I let it go. The story, told so nonchalantly, made me sad. It seemed that Allegra had always used sex as somewhat of a weapon, a game, or a means to an end. It made me wonder if what had just happened in the bathroom meant anything at all. Did she really want to be with me, or was she just killing time or trying to get something she wanted?

She turned onto her side to face me and started tracing shapes on my skin with her index finger. When she kissed me, I quickly abandoned those doubtful thoughts. This was different. *We* were different. It wouldn't feel like this if she weren't sincere.

When she pulled away, Allegra said, "I love you too."

"Do you mean that?"

"Of course I do," she said. She looked me straight in the eye and there wasn't a single hint of regret in her voice.

When she had told me about all the boys she'd dated, hooked up with, whatever, there had never been this air of certainty. She hadn't loved any of them, but she loved me. Allegra Elizabeth Long, the most beautiful girl I had ever met, loved me too. With those four words, she had given me everything. 'Wonderstruck' doesn't even begin to cover how I felt.

Ally kissed me again, guiding my shoulders until I laid on my side, facing her. After it left my shoulder, her left hand settled on the back of my neck. It reminded me of the first time we had kissed, months before at my dad's house.

I started to feel sleepy, eyelids drooping and breath becoming more regular. I let my mind drift where it pleased, and eventually remembered that Ally wanted my help to kill someone. My brain finally finished processing the idea, wrapping all the way around it. I didn't want to hurt someone, and I didn't want to end up in prison, but I did want Allegra. She was all I wanted, and this would help me keep her.

I fought against the heavy blanket of sleep trying to envelop me like a cocoon and looked her in the eyes.

"Okay," I said. "I'm ready to hear the plan again."

CHAPTER 11

Allegra

February 2008

The plan was simple, really.

Step zero: Get Robin on board. If she wasn't already convinced, it would be easy to talk her into it over a few weeks of gentle prodding.

Step one: Call my mom and ask to take a tour of her facility. I was taking an anthropology class at the community college, and there really was a unit about homelessness, so it wasn't too far-fetched to tell her it was for a school assignment.

Step two: Make friends with one of the kids who lives there. Preferably a boy, preferably not too young. This was the victim profile that I knew Robin would grow the least attached to, therefore, it held the smallest chance of her getting spooked and backing out. Give the kid my number before leaving.

Step three: Wait for the kid to call or text me. Whether he needs help or he's looking for a date, it shouldn't be more than a few weeks before he tries to contact me. When he does, invite him over to hang out with Robin and me.

Step four: Spike his drink with something that will make him pass out. I didn't have any animal tranquilizers à la Karla Homolka, so NyQuil or something would have to suffice.

Step five: Tie him up while he's passed out, kill him when he wakes up. It was important not to plan this part out too much. It would be better if it was a little spontaneous. I just had to remember a plastic sheet so we didn't ruin the carpet in the apartment.

Step six: Dismember the body and dissolve it with lye powder. Lye powder is surprisingly easy to get; it comes in gallon jars at Home Depot because it's good at breaking down biological tissue (hair, dead skin), so people use it to unclog their drains. If you've ever seen Fight Club, you know it'll leave a nasty wound on human skin when mixed with moisture. That thing Tyler Durden does to Jack's hand? I planned to do that to an entire corpse.

My mom sounded surprised when I identified myself on the phone. I guess it had been a while since we'd talked. I hardly remembered to interact with my family now that I no longer lived with them.

"Hey, Mom, how's it going?"

"Um… Good. Fine. How's independent life?"

"It's okay. School and stuff, you know." I wasn't in the mood to feign small talk, so I navigated to the purpose of my call as quickly as possible. "I actually had a question for you."

"You need money?" she asked, sounding burdened. It was a fair assumption with my out-of-the-blue call.

"No, I actually have an assignment I was hoping you could help me with. We're doing a unit on homelessness in one of my classes, and it's extra credit to tour a facility and write about it."

"Ooh, extra credit." She sounded cautiously optimistic about the prospect, probably recalling that I had literally never gone the extra mile for a school assignment before. I hoped she wouldn't think this was suspiciously out-of-character behavior, but I'd been right to depend on the blind spot all parents have for academic excellence.

We set up a time for her to pick Robin and me up at our apartment and take us to work with her for the day. I didn't really want to spend the entire day there, but without our own car, it seemed like the only option.

Step one: Complete.

The day finally arrived for us to tour Mom's facility in Cave Creek. It was a full two weeks after the morning I tried to tell Robin the plan, but it had felt like so much longer. My cell phone alarm blared at an ungodly 7:30 a.m. We had fallen asleep, naked and deliciously entangled, less than four hours before. Now I had to put on makeup and pretend I was whoever my mom thought I was.

Next to me, Robin groaned loudly. "What in the actual fuck is that fucking thing doing *chiming* like that?" she yelled.

"I know, I know," I said, hitting the red button and basking in the silence that followed. I stood up and moved the window curtain aside half an inch, then squinted in disgust at the bright rays that streamed in. "Don't look outside unless you want your retinas to burn. My mom will be here in about half an hour to pick us up."

"Fuuuuuuck!" Robin whined, flailing as she pulled the comforter up over her head.

"You're very foul before nine," I told her, smirking.

"Yeah, and why *aren't* you?"

I shrugged even though she was still hiding under the blanket and couldn't see me. "I don't know. Excited, I guess. You know. It's a big day."

"It's a day," she muttered.

I pounced onto the bed on my hands and knees, pulled the comforter down to Robin's shoulders, and gave her a long, drawn-out kiss on the cheek. "I'm gonna make coffee. If I promise to put some in a to-go cup for you, will you get up and get dressed?"

Robin squeezed her eyes shut and pretended to ignore me, but she still grinned at the kiss. As I climbed off the bed and shimmied into a flowy blouse and yesterday's jeans, she grumbled in what I assumed to be agreement.

I started the coffee dripping and then retreated to the bathroom to make my hair shine and cover my face in expertly applied foundation, blush, and shadow. This was partially for my mom, to show her that I'm just as self-centered and self-obsessed as ever and couldn't possibly be bothered to have ulterior motives for this visit. It was also so I could attract the type of boy who would be too busy trying to look down my shirt to notice that my spare bedroom was full of plastic and rope. After completing my hair and makeup, I stared at the finished product in the bathroom mirror until I decided to switch the blouse for a tight, hot pink tank top. The color helped emphasize my cheeks and lips, and it clung to each of my curves while showing off a fair amount of cleavage. As a final touch, I threw on a black hoodie and zipped it almost to the top. This way, the boy would think what he saw was a secret for his eyes only.

I bounced back into the kitchen. Robin leaned against the counter, sipping from a reusable plastic travel mug with a Starbucks logo. Her hair still needed to be brushed, but she was wearing jeans and a t-shirt and already had shoes on. "This is ridiculous. I haven't been up this early since high school."

"It's for a good cause."

Robin made her way to the bathroom without answering.

My mom pulled into the parking lot of the apartment complex at exactly eight o'clock. She had been insistent that we shouldn't leave a minute later than that since she wasn't used to driving to work from my place and we didn't know how long it would take to drive thirty-five miles in rush hour traffic. I personally thought it was stupid to allot an hour to a drive we all knew wouldn't take that long, but I put my criticism aside in favor of the bigger picture.

"Good morning!" my mom chirped as Robin and I climbed into her gray sedan. She wore one of her signature dark pantsuits and no makeup, her curly hair glinting almost orange as the sun reflected off all the car mirrors.

"Hi," I answered. Robin grunted into her coffee.

The ride took about fifty minutes. When we hit the forty-five-minute mark, I identified a three-car pileup as the reason traffic had slowed to a crawl. I thought about making a sarcastic comment about how Mom's obsessive planning ahead had actually paid off this time, but decided against it in favor of keeping the peace. I just wish I had seen the crash happen. As we got closer to the facility, my mom shifted into work mode and started listing everything on her schedule for the day.

"I don't have any staff meetings today, so it's actually a good day for you to visit. I'll show you around first thing, so you know where everything is. There's a small group at eleven, and it's just arts and crafts so you'll be able to observe. After lunch, we can sit down, and you can ask me questions for your report. I might even be able to get my supervisor in on that if she's not too busy today. Then there's a small counseling group at three, which, unfortunately, you can't observe because of confidentiality, but you're welcome to walk around and look at things on your own during that if you want." She paused for a few seconds, possibly waiting for me to respond.

"Cool," I said, nodding. "Sounds like you planned it perfectly."

"Well, I'm excited that you wanted to come and see Foundation House. I've worked there practically your whole life and you've never shown an interest before."

"There's a first time for everything," Robin piped up. I don't think my mom noticed the sarcasm in her cliché statement, but I was not amused. If my mom figured out that I was lying about the school project, she'd demand answers and wouldn't accept my usual method of side-stepping the truth or distracting her with a change of subject. I knew this wasn't exactly Robin's idea of fun, but she wouldn't dare try to derail the plan—would she?

We pulled into a large dirt parking lot and Mom found a spot near the main office of Foundation House. I got out of the car and surveyed what I could see of the facility through my pink sunglasses. Several single-story adobe buildings stood baking in the early morning sun. Three horses stood in a pen between two of the buildings, clouds of dust and flies visible around them even from a distance. A dirt path led from the horse pen to the main road, where I assumed a riding trail began. I also smelled what could only be the air from cafeteria vents, cluing me in that there was a canteen somewhere nearby.

"It looks like a mini summer camp," I told my mom as she got out of the car.

She beamed as she shouldered her bag. "It is looking good these days, isn't it? I got a grant for those horses. The first ten years I worked here, we had an empty stable. So useless. So one day I said, 'I'm gonna fill it up!'"

Robin stumbled out of the backseat, chugging the rest of her coffee so she could leave the cup in the car. I straightened her t-shirt, which was wrinkled from the ride and twisted around her torso. Her hand covered mine and she tried to interlace our fingers, but I dropped my hand before she could. As I turned to face my mom, I caught the disappointed look on Robin's face out the corner of my eye.

We followed Mom across the parking lot and into a building marked *Admin*. She led us into a tiny office with generic desert paintings on three of its four tan walls, dropping her bag onto the swivel chair and setting her thermos on the desk.

"So, how many kids come here during the day?" I asked.

"Just drop your stuff anywhere, girls," she said distractedly. "We only have about ten kids who come in the mornings during the school year. They're usually already graduated, dropouts, or ditching for the day. The high schoolers start to trickle in around two."

Back outside, Mom showed us around the three buildings and the outdoor space. We saw the various classrooms they used for instructional programs, the space reminiscent of a hotel ballroom where large gatherings were held, and the small enclave of apartments where the residents of the youth housing program lived. We also met the three horses (Nino, Pinto, and Saint Mario, named from a group poll after the grant to buy them had come through) and walked through the cafeteria where they were already starting to prepare lunch. Finally, we were shown the bathrooms, emergency exits, and the fire door that would set off an alarm if opened without a key.

The eleven a.m. arts and crafts group felt like a total flop. Only three "kids" showed up, two boys and a girl around my age. All three of them looked like the only reason they were there was because they were given the choice between making a plastic lanyard or going to jail. Maybe they had been. They were all too old and too uninterested to be of any use to me. I tied a few messy knots in my pieces of plastic. When Robin showed me her perfectly spiraled keychain design at the end of the hour, I couldn't believe what a beautiful object she'd made in such a short time. I forgot until after lunch that as a knitter, she produced beautiful things all the time.

I faked my interview with my mom pretty well, if I do say so myself. I had spent some time the previous evening searching the internet for Career Day–type questions, knowing I just had to lead Mom in the direction of talking about her work and she would fill the quiet office for the better part of an hour. I was right; she babbled on about the horses, after-school classes, summer workshops, and continuously being able to grow the housing program because of grants and significant community donations.

"The community out here really seems to believe in what we're doing," she gushed.

I nodded, taking notes on the legal pad she had let me borrow. Robin sat in an armless plastic chair in the corner, legs crossed and eyes trained on my mom. I couldn't tell if she was a great actor or much more interested in my mom's work than I was.

During the afternoon therapy group, Robin and I wandered the grounds. We kicked up clouds of dust with our sneakers that settled on our jeans and the fine hair on our arms. The campus seemed to have woken up in the afternoon. There were now probably thirty high-school-age kids heading in different directions toward a snack, a counselor, their apartment, or a quiet place to do homework. I stayed vigilant as we crossed a small courtyard, looking for someone who fit the victim profile I had meticulously created.

A teen boy in baggy jeans and a blue polo shirt slumped onto a bench at the far end of the courtyard. His blonde hair partially obscured his face, but I could see brown eyes and freckles before he turned his head away from me. He opened his black backpack and started rifling through it, aggressively searching for something. After about thirty seconds, he triumphantly pulled out an energy drink in a plastic bottle and took a celebratory swig. I felt someone watching me and turned to see Robin trying to bore a hole through my temple with a laser-focused, intense stare.

"What?" I asked innocently.

Robin rolled her eyes. "Is that him?" she asked with a sharp edge in her voice.

"Well, I don't know," I said playfully, basking in her annoyance. "Why don't we go ask him."

She shook her head, but then surprised me by being the first to start walking in his direction. By the time I approached the bench, she had already sat down and introduced herself.

"Hey," he said when I came over. "I'm Bruce. Are you guys new here?"

"Nah," I said, squinting in the sun despite the pink sunglasses I'd put on again when we came outside. "Just here for the day, taking a tour for school."

Bruce nodded, seeming satisfied with that explanation. I was glad I wouldn't have to go into who my mom was, needlessly identifying my familial connection with someone he probably knew.

"Do you live here?" Robin asked. I cringed internally at her bluntness, even though I knew it was important information.

Again, Bruce seemed unphased. "Sometimes," he said, "but not officially." He took another breath like he was going to add more information, but thought better of it at the last minute.

The three of us talked for a few more minutes about useless things like the hot, dry, predictable weather and why Bruce didn't feel like going to any structured groups that afternoon. After some gentle prodding, I found out that he was telling the staff he had a family member to stay with but was really hopping between park benches when the weather was nice, enclosed plastic bus stations when it wasn't, and friends' couches when he got exceptionally lucky. When Robin asked about his parents, he shrugged and mumbled something about them not understanding him. When I asked if he was dating anyone, he blushed a deep crimson and his freckles momentarily disappeared. He had run away from Pennsylvania eight months ago, leaving his cell phone and ID behind. He now used a pay-as-you-go phone to call and text who he wanted without his parents being able to track him. He was seventeen.

Eventually, Robin excused herself to use the bathroom. I scooted closer to Bruce, unzipping my sweatshirt subtly while in motion. I felt the slight breeze on my collar bones and noticed Bruce trying not to notice my newly exposed cleavage. We had already established that Bruce was semi-homeless, didn't have any relatives in the state, and didn't have a significant other who would wonder where he went—three huge green lights illuminating him as the perfect subject. This was the final test, seeing if I could lure him in with lust the way I'd attracted and used guys in the past. This wouldn't work if the reason his parents "didn't understand him" was because he was gay, which my mom had informed me earlier resulted in over half of teen runaways in the country. I stood up and adjusted my clothes, pulling the neckline of the tank top right to the top hem of my black bra and pretending not to notice, then sat back on the bench.

"It must be the hottest part of the day," I said, slipping the hoodie down to my elbows so my chest and shoulders could catch some sunlight. Behind my sunglasses, I watched Bruce's line of sight as he glanced at my just-barely exposed bra, then quickly away. He busied himself by rooting through his backpack again.

I tried again to engage him in conversation. "So, what kind of stuff do you like to do?"

He shrugged. "Nothing much, really. Hang out. Skateboard. Video games when I can, but I don't, like, have my own system or anything."

I nodded thoughtfully. An idea formed quickly in my head, and it was so perfect I had to blurt it out before I had time to second guess myself. "Well, we have a PS3 if you ever want to come over and play."

"That sounds cool. What kind of games do you have?"

I rattled off a few games that I remembered Toby occasionally playing, and knew I had their titles right when Bruce nodded more enthusiastically and even broke into a smile.

"Hell yeah, I'd love to come play with you! Wait…" His face fell from excited to suspicious, and I momentarily worried about the impossibility that he had psychically figured out my whole plan. "This is too good to be true. There must be a catch."

"No catch," I said. "As long as you can make your way to Tempe."

"And there it is," Bruce said, sounding disappointed. His voice even cracked a little, betraying how recently it had dropped into a lower register. "How am I supposed to get all the way to Tempe without a ride or my own car?"

I shrug, allowing my chest to bounce more than necessary on the way down. "I'll give you my number, and I guess if you want to play with me badly enough, you'll figure out how to get there."

Bruce blushed again as he caught my incredibly obvious double entendre. High school boys were so easy.

Robin walked back across the courtyard toward us as Bruce handed me his green spiral biology notebook and I wrote my name and cell number inside the front cover. He looked at what I wrote, then gazed up at me through his blonde bangs. "Nice to meet you, Allegra."

"We should probably go back to the office," Robin said, addressing me and ignoring Bruce.

I took my cell phone out of my pocket to check the time and was surprised to see it was almost time for Mom to be off work.

"Shit," I said, "you're right. Bye, Bruce."

I stood up and followed Robin back to the Admin building, looking back only once to make sure Bruce was watching my hips swing in my tight jeans as I walked away. He was, so I looked over the top of my pink glasses and gave him a quick wink before slipping through the double doors.

When we got inside, I took Robin by the shoulders in celebration. "I think that was it. Holy shit, I think we did it. I can't believe we did what we came here for."

"What do you mean?" she sneered. "That was literally the whole point of coming here."

"I know, but a little part of me didn't actually believe we'd succeed. It's like being five years old and saying you want to be a doctor when you grow up. Sure, you *want* to be a doctor, but will you really put yourself through eight years of medical school when it's time to commit? I guess I just didn't think the stars would align perfectly enough that we'd actually be able to pull off our plan!"

I was breathless from all the words fighting to escape my throat at the same time. I kissed Robin on the mouth, soft and lingering, and only when I pulled back did she smile.

CHAPTER 12

Robin

February 2008

The drive home from Cave Creek was quiet except for the rush of air whooshing through my slightly lowered back window. Over lunch, I'd taken the opportunity to apologize to Ally's mom for being so antisocial on the drive there that morning, using the early hour and my addictive need to ingest caffeine as an excuse. She had accepted immediately, assuring me no apology was necessary, and we'd spent the rest of the day making pleasant small talk. Now that the day was rapidly disappearing into evening, I could tell the only reason she wasn't continuing our friendly banter was because she was tired. Bright rays of sun glared harshly through the windshield as it set. The three of us faced it, squinting, wishing we were already home.

The car pulled into our complex parking lot, and we both thanked Ally's mom for the ride and for showing us how her facility worked.

"Why don't you girls come over for dinner sometime soon?" she shouted after us as we climbed out. We promised we would.

I extracted my keyring from my front pocket and unlocked the door, then immediately went into my room and closed the door. This was something I never did. After sitting down on my bed, I tried to remember the last time that door had been closed without us being in here together. I came up blank.

Of course, Allegra didn't get the message. I heard two thumps as she kicked her shoes off in the living room. Then she approached the bedroom door, pausing for only a second or two before turning the knob and letting herself in.

"Okay, I already know you're mad, and I already know *why* you're mad, so let's just get it over with so we can make out."

I let my head drop forward and cradled my forehead in one hand. "I'm not mad," I insisted. "Just tired. It was a long day and we got up so early. Can we please just go to bed?"

"No, that's ridiculous. It's like, seven p.m." Allegra said curtly. "Now come on, out with it. You're mad at me for flirting with that Bruce kid. What kind of a name is that anyway? Bruuuuce…" She over-emphasized the name, drawing it out and then trailing off as she waited for me to answer.

"I swear I'm not *mad*. It was just different actually seeing the plan in action, that's all."

"You're damn right it was different. It was better!"

"Maybe for you. Not for me."

It might have been my imagination, but I thought I saw Allegra's combative body language soften a little as she considered what I'd said. She sat in front of me on the bed and mirrored my criss-cross-apple-sauce position.

"You know none of it means anything," she said. "All that today, it was just a means to an end."

My face flashed a sarcastic expression meant to convey, *Oh really?* Then I pulled my t-shirt off and used my upper arms to push my breasts together inside my blue sports bra. In a mocking Betty Boop tone, I said, "Oooh, Bruuuce, look at meeee! Get distracted by my perfect cleavage and never mind why I, a beautiful college student, would even look twice at you, let alone keep up a ten-minute conversation about video games and other pointless bullshit!"

"Oh, right," Allegra said, snapping her fingers as she remembered. "Video games. We have to borrow Toby's PS3 so we have something to do with Bruce before he passes out."

"Why aren't you taking me seriously?" I asked loudly. I relaxed my arms and leaned back against the bed pillows, defeated.

"Because you can't possibly *be* serious," Allegra said in the same non-chalant tone she'd been using since we got home. "Finding a victim and flirting to get him here was literally the entire reason we went today. You knew that. Why are you mad now?"

"I told you, it was different seeing it happening right in front of me."

"Well, you need to get over that because he's definitely going to text me. This is supposed to be fun, remember?"

"Whatever, I give up." I desperately wanted to change the subject, but something she'd said a few minutes before had piqued my curiosity. "Why do we need Toby's PS3?"

"Because I told Bruce we have a PS3."

"No, I mean, why bother *actually* having a PS3? That's just bait to get him here, then when he's here tell him it's in the shop or something."

"'In the shop.'" Allegra mused at my wording, smirking and looking absently down at the comforter.

"Or wherever you take video game systems to be repaired. I've never touched a controller in my life. Although, the thought of me trying to beat people up in Grand Theft Auto is pretty entertaining."

"I mean, I guess that could work. But what if he gets pissed and leaves?"

"Ally. He's seventeen and you're inviting him here to get drunk with two cute older girls. It's literally a straight teen boy's dream. Even if he *does* get here and there's no video games, I don't think he'll go anywhere."

She cracked up laughing at this because she knew it was true.

We settled into the pillows, and I picked up my knitting as she reached for the TV remote. I was still working on her light gray scarf. It was a little over five feet long now, and I had about half a skein of yarn still to use. Some prime time celebrity competition that neither of us had ever followed played at low volume on the TV. Allegra inhaled as if she was about to speak, but then relaxed again and kept her eyes on the screen. The show cut to commercial.

"Were you about to say something?" I asked.

She shifted her body to face me. "Yeah, I was just wondering… You're not *really* mad at me for flirting with Bruce, are you?"

"Would it change anything if I were?"

"Yes." She paused then to consider, but nodded her head and reiterated, "Yeah, of course it would."

I sigh heavily and locked my eyes on my rapidly moving fingers and the construction of each fuzzy woven row of yarn. "I told you I'm not mad. It just hurt my feelings, that's all. I know it was because of *The Plan*," I stress the words to give them the reverence I knew Allegra felt they deserved, "but seeing you purposefully try to attract someone else was almost too much. I really hated it. I don't want to see it again."

My needles clinked in time with TV commercial jingles until I decided to bind off the scarf at its current length. I knitted the final row, cast off, and snipped the end of the yarn with the small pair of scissors I kept on my bedside table. I handed the scarf to Allegra, an unceremonious presentation of the gift she had already known was coming. She took it with both hands and fidgeted with it in her lap as she spoke.

"I didn't do any of that today to make you jealous, or to make you doubt us. He is a teeny tiny baby child. I have no interest in Bruce besides tying the little twerp up and watching him beg for his life."

"I know," I said, my voice wavering.

"Do you?" Allegra set the scarf next to us on the bed as she waited for my answer. I shifted my eyes up from it to her concerned face, still accented with symmetrical wings of eyeliner and dabs of blush perfectly blended to appear invisible. "Robin. You are the only one for me. I love you."

I wasn't sure I could believe her after the world-class performance she had put on for Bruce earlier that day, but my uncertainty was a blip in my brain compared to the magnificent fireworks that boomed in my head every time I heard her say those three little words. She tugged on my arm until I joined her in lying down. I positioned my head on her chest and listened to her heartbeat, getting lost in the thub-thub, thub-thub, thub-thub until I lost track of time.

Long after the sun had set, she came back from the bathroom in nothing but a pair of cotton briefs, helped me undress, and buried her face between my legs until my body convulsed and tears streamed down my face. When I recovered, we piled paper plates with sandwiches and chips in the kitchen and brought them back to bed to eat while watching a late-night rerun of *Leave It to Beaver*. It felt so normal, I almost forgot what our disagreement had been about in the first place. Of course she wanted only me. She loved me. How could I have doubted that?

CHAPTER 13

Allegra

February 2008

Walking into my high school dance room the Monday after our visit to Foundation House was like time-warping one year into the past. Ashley the Overachiever and Yessenia the Gymnast were both still going to school here, a sophomore and a senior respectively, so I even recognized some faces. They both grinned and waved at me when I entered the room as if we'd been best friends the previous year. There were four other girls whose names I forgot as soon as they introduced themselves. The varsity dance team had six members this year, more than I'd ever seen as a student.

Andrea bounced over to me with her usual sunny disposition. "Allegra, so glad you made it!" she bubbled. I smiled back, still trying to fit back into my unfamiliar dance team persona. It was Monday at 3:30, and I was reporting for duty as a guest choreographer.

Admittedly, I hadn't done a lot of advance preparation for this class. Aside from choosing the song they would dance to (an upbeat remix of "I Will Possess Your Heart" by Death Cab for Cutie), I hadn't actually planned anything. Luckily, Andrea led the six girls in a few warm-up exercises and stretches, giving me time to listen to the song on my iPod a couple of times and write down a few steps and formations for them to try.

"All right, girls," Andrea announced when the stretching was over and everyone was taking a water break. "Some of you know her, but we have a very special guest for our first alumni choreographer. Please welcome Allegra Long!"

There was a smattering of distracted applause as the team looked me over, assessing whether it would be worth their time to listen to me. I hoped Yessenia and Ashley would vouch for me, at least enough that the other girls would be quiet while I was teaching if not retain the material from week to week.

I wanted not to care if they liked me, not to care whether my dance turned out well at the end, but the truth was, I wanted to do a good job. I had stuck with the dance team for three years of high school because I loved performing. I never would have admitted it aloud, but I was excited to be back dancing on this gross marley floor and checking the lines and shapes my body made in the smudged floor-to-ceiling mirrors. I'm sure that any more than an hour a week would have felt like overkill, but for the moment, I was glad to be there.

"Hi, everyone," I addressed the group when the light applause died down. "I just graduated last year, so hi to those of you that I know. Um… I'll start out by playing you the song we'll be using. While you listen, feel free to do some improv. However the music makes you feel like moving is great. I'll watch and maybe pick up some of your moves to put into our dance."

This was an activity I had historically enjoyed in Andrea's class and others. I could tell by the students' facial expressions that they didn't totally hate the idea. I played the song three times and alternated between writing down steps I saw some girls use and trying out some new ones of my own. During the next water break, I visited my purse and flipped open my cell phone to check for messages. I only had one, from a number I didn't recognize: *hey is this allegra?*

Maybe, who's this? I responded.

The response made my phone buzz just as I was about to return my phone to my purse and continue with the dance class. *it's bruce… i might be able to find a ride to tempe if u still wanna hang out.*

I seriously considered pretending not to remember him, but I wasn't sure if that would make him more interested or confuse him until he decided not to bother. I answered quickly, letting him know I was busy but would get back to him later.

I hardly paid attention to what I was teaching for the rest of the class, my mind was spinning with so many gruesome possibilities. I mentally reviewed my list for the hardware store which included lye, plastic sheeting, extra buckets, and whichever tools looked like the most fun. How would I react when I had a real person in front of me begging for his life? Would I cower and fail, even after all my mental preparation, or would I get too excited and bite him on the ass out of sheer adrenaline like Bundy in the sorority house? Should I draw out the torture, reviving him every time he passed out the way Gacy played with his little boys? I was surprised when Andrea tapped me on the shoulder, knocking me out of my reverie to let me know that my sixty minutes were over and she'd see me next week.

I took an alternate bus route on the way home so I could stop at Home Depot. I literally hated this store more than anything in existence, from the impossible-to-navigate aisles to the glaring orange apron sported by every employee. Rather than ask anyone for help and be accosted up close by the overwhelming tangerine, I took my time wandering up and down every aisle with my oversized shopping cart. I tossed in four packages of plastic sheeting, a six-pack of packing tape, a box of one hundred tiny utility knife replacement blades, two rolls of standard weight nylon rope, a lightweight hacksaw that advertised an easy grip, and a beginner's toolkit. I also grabbed a stack of medium cardboard boxes to go with the tape, so the cashier would assume I was buying all this stuff for some kind of construction project or big move.

I found gallon-size buckets of sodium hydroxide, aka lye, when I was almost finished shopping. The hardest part of the day would be lugging this thing home on the bus. The brightly colored label advertised that the solution was perfect for unclogging drains, which meant it could dissolve tissue. I knew from discreet research and carefully asked questions in high school chemistry class that combining lye with water in a closed container would break down anything organic that you tossed in. I also knew it wouldn't eat through the bathtub as long as the solution was properly diluted because it was frequently used as a deep-cleaning product when the regular-strength stuff wouldn't suffice.

On the bus again, the gallon of lye vibrating between my feet with the movement of the road, I decided I had left Bruce hanging long enough. I opened my phone and texted him back. I told him to come over Friday night at seven and gave our address. I told him to bring booze if he could, not because I thought he actually would, but just to get him wondering what naughty things besides underage drinking might be on the table.

I unlocked our apartment door and stepped inside, my face was flushed with the effort of carrying the gallon bucket and my other bags from the bus stop. Robin was cross-legged on the living room couch with knitting needles in her lap. Her eyes widened as she watched me drop the bags and bucket onto the floor.

"Let me guess," she said, her lips tightening into a hard, thin line. "He texted you?"

"Yeah! It's happening Friday. Will you help me get this stuff into the spare room?"

Plastic sheeting covered the floor, dresser, and bare mattress in the spare room, secured at the edges with packing tape. A tall floor lamp loomed ominously in the corner, the only light source. The saw, toolkit, rope, and razor blades were all unwrapped and laid out on the mattress, ready. A wadded pair of lime green socks from my dresser, to be used as a gag, completed the pile of tools. Three bottles of wine and one bottle of vodka were lined up on the kitchen counter. I'd relocated a bottle of NyQuil from the bathroom to a hiding place in one of the kitchen cabinets for easy access when I made him a drink. By the time Robin woke up on Friday morning, everything was set up. She carried out her morning routine without questioning the little changes I had made to our apartment. She had to work an afternoon shift, and wouldn't come home until after Bruce was already at our place. She left around two in the afternoon with a quick kiss on the lips and very little conversation.

After she went to work, I sat on the floor in the spare room and examined the contents of the toolkit. Inside the sleek black case, forty shiny pieces sparkled in the dim overhead light. Even with useless items like the tape measure and driving bits, there were several promising tools nestled into their perfectly shaped compartments. I tested the weight of the hammer, even tapping it on the carpeted floor a few times like a judge's gavel. I didn't think I would use this until the very end, if at all. I made sure the utility knife, pliers, and both screwdrivers were easily accessible before closing the case and leaving the room in perfect order.

I spent the majority of the afternoon making myself look magnificent. In the shower, I shaved my legs and underarms, conditioned my hair twice, and applied a gritty deep-cleansing masque to my face. When I got out, I brushed my hair straight while blasting it with the blow dryer until it resembled a platinum waterfall. Unlike the day we toured Foundation House, I went with a natural makeup look with just a little gray eyeshadow and no eyeliner. I dressed in a red and black striped dress I'd had for a couple of years but rarely worn. It was cut low in the front and the panels covering my breasts were loose and blousy. The skirt clung to my thighs, cutting off just above my knees. It made me feel so powerful that I didn't even want to pair it with shoes. I decided the ultimate power move would be going barefoot. After the rest of me was ready, I painted my finger- and toenails bright red to match the dress's stripes.

On my way to the kitchen to triple-check that everything was ready, the scarf Robin had made for me caught my eye. It was draped over the corner of her dresser, one end dangling almost to the floor. I impulsively picked it up and wrapped it twice around my neck. It didn't go with my outfit at all, but the feathery yarn was soft against my skin. As the scarf started to warm my neck and chest, it occurred to me how cold the AC made our little apartment. I approached the thermostat planning to turn it up, but then remembered that cold was better for the activities I had planned. I adjusted the temperature to five degrees cooler and wrapped the scarf a little tighter around my neck.

Around six, I started drinking wine. I wasn't nervous exactly, but first times always came with a little apprehension of the unknown. I was almost done with the first bottle by the time Bruce sent a message asking which apartment number was mine. I flung the scarf onto the arm of the couch and answered the door with a wine bottle in my hand. Bruce stood there with the same backpack, hoodie, and floppy yellow hair as when we met. He just stared for a few seconds, as if trying to decide whether he had the right apartment. He grabbed the waistband of his baggy jeans and hitched them up.

"Holy shit. Are you having a party?" he asked, looking from my dress to the bottle and back.

"No, silly," I answered, pulling him across the threshold by the wrist and closing the door. "It's just us for now. My roommate will be home from work a little later. Have a seat. Do you want a drink?"

Bruce crossed the room and flopped onto the couch, backpack landing at his feet. The way he ambled reminded me of how young he was. "Um, sure," he said. "What do you have?"

"Wine, vodka, and a variety of mixers. Preference?"

"I've actually never had wine *or* vodka," Bruce said sheepishly.

I grinned, both because I thought this was adorable and because he wouldn't know what either was supposed to taste like, making hiding the NyQuil that much easier. "I'll surprise you," I said as I slipped into the kitchen.

I mixed him a drink consisting of vodka, orange juice, a full dose of NyQuil, and a splash of red wine to confuse the taste and color. I stirred it for longer than necessary, careful to dissolve the viscous green-blue medicine completely in the rest of the liquid. I made myself the same drink, without the secret ingredient, and made sure to hand him the correct glass.

We sat and talked for a while, long enough that he drained his drink and I made him another one. I learned a lot about the politics of popularity at the high school he had left behind in Pennsylvania and got the impression that Bruce wasn't among the social elite. He also couldn't stop mentioning how happy he was to be out of there now and "rid of that stupid place forever." He was putting on a bravado for me, flirting with me, and, in a way, already thought he was guaranteed to get at least one hand down my pants because I had invited him into my apartment, gotten drunk, and laughed at his jokes. I encouraged this line of thinking, watching his confidence inflate every time I nodded contemplatively at something he said or pseudo-obliviously adjusted my legs so he could see a little farther up my skirt.

"So," Bruce said, setting his half-finished second drink on the coffee table Robin and I had found at a yard sale the week after moving in. "Do you have a boyfriend?"

I stopped myself from snorting into my drink and instead hid my smirk with the glass. "No, I don't. Why do you ask?"

"Well, you asked the other day if I'm seeing anyone. I was just curious about you." His face was pink and flushed from the drink and the question. He picked up his drink again and chugged the rest in one gulp.

"Why, Bruce? Do you have someone you want to set me up with?" I stood up and took a few steps toward him until I was directly in front of him, staring him down.

He blinked several times at me as if what I'd said didn't make any sense. "Not exactly, I…"

His speech had become noticeably slower and clumsier in the last few minutes. I knelt next to the couch and took his glass so he didn't drop it on the carpet. I stayed on my knees and looked up at him with puppy dog eyes. Slowly, I put one hand on each of his ankles and drew my index fingers up the inseam of his jeans.

"Or, did you mean yourself? Were you hoping that you'd come over here, and I'd get into this exact position, and then maybe you'd find yourself with your dick in my mouth?" My fingers ended their journey at his zipper, where they lingered for a few seconds before dropping back to my sides.

In my experience, boys all responded differently to this kind of direct confrontation. Some backed down and apologized. Others took it as a challenge, an opportunity to get assertive. Bruce was rapidly becoming sleepier and I wanted to inspire some kind of reaction before he passed out, so I had to encourage it just a little bit more. I stood up and placed one knee on each side of him so that I was straddling his lap.

"What are you doing?" He asked in disbelief.

I leaned forward and whispered in his ear, "Isn't this what you came for?"

His eyes closed for longer than a blink and I could tell it took effort to open them again. Slowly, tentatively, Bruce put his hands on my torso. I guided one up and into the red and black folds of fabric covering my chest. I slid his other hand down and under the hem of my dress. He perked up with a tiny surge of adrenaline as one of his fingers slipped inside me. He gasped and moaned a little in my ear. His eyes fell closed again.

"Bruce?" I whispered.

"Hmm…" he responded absently. It might not have been a response at all, just a dreamy hum as he drifted off.

"Bruce, I'm going to move you to the murder room now," I whispered, disengaging from both of his hands and standing up. "And don't worry, I won't even tell my girlfriend that you penetrated me. It'll be our little secret." I winked at his unconscious form on the couch, then opened the door of the spare room and grabbed the rope.

•———

"Why are you wearing a party dress?"

This was the first thing Robin asked when she got home, which wasn't that weird until I considered the scene she was walking into. I had Bruce stripped naked and tied him up in a sitting position on the floor against the mattress in the spare room, the rolled-up socks in his mouth. He wasn't fully awake yet so I was waiting, hammer in one hand and scissors in the other in case he suddenly revived and tried to make a run for it. I had no idea if my knots would hold him. They weren't the important part.

"I knew it was too much," I said without turning toward her. "It felt like a special occasion, I wanted to look hot."

"You do," Robin said sincerely, staring at me from the living room.

I came out to meet her, leaving the hammer and scissors on the floor out of Bruce's reach with the rest of my supplies. "You really think?" I asked, twirling on my way to give her a kiss.

"Of course I do." She peered over my shoulder to catch another glimpse of Bruce, incapacitated on the floor. "Is he okay? How long has he been here?"

"He got here right on time," I bragged, stepping out of the doorway and closing Bruce into the room by himself. "Poor little guy passed out after only double the recommended dose of NyQuil and four shots of vodka."

"I'm gonna take a shower."

"Wait, just shower later. I have him all ready for us."

"I can see that. What do you even want me to do? I told you gore isn't really my thing. I'm literally just here because you want me to be."

I shrugged and danced around in front of her impatiently, like a toddler who had to go potty. "I don't know, come help me. You can do whatever you want to him. It's a good opportunity to get your anger out."

"That's why I knit," Robin said with a smirk.

She followed me to the kitchen and watched as I mixed up another cocktail for our guest. "Do you want one? I'll make yours like mine, without the night-night juice."

Robin poured half an inch of vodka into a clean glass, took the shot with her head tossed back, and winced as she swallowed. "I might need more of this to get to sleep tonight. Don't use it all."

When she put the glass down, I grabbed her hands and held them tightly in mine. "I know you're not necessarily thrilled that Bruce is here—"

"I don't care that he's here, it's—"

"It's *why* he's here, I know," I finished the sentence for her, parroting the same thing she had said every time I brought up his visit since finalizing it on Monday. "I know you're not necessarily thrilled, but this is the coolest thing I've ever done, and you helped make it happen. Will you please, please come in there with me?"

She still looked unsure.

"You don't even need to stay until…you know. The end."

"I just need a few minutes. I'll be in." She smiled, but her eyes were worried. She slipped through our bedroom door and closed it behind her.

I went back to Bruce, whose eyelids were starting to flutter. I sat next to him and slapped his cheeks a few times, calling his name until he perked up and focused on me. I picked up two screwdrivers that fit completely in the palm of my hand. I considered jamming one through his eye, but that felt too dramatic for so early in the night. Instead, I felt for two of his ribs and jammed the flat head into the space between. There was a soft pop as the skin gave way, and then a trickle of dark blood dripped over his skin and pooled on the plastic. Bruce grunted violently with the force and his eyes slammed open, awake and alert.

"Good, you're awake. If you don't scream, I'll take out your gag. Okay? Understand?"

He nodded, pressing himself into the side of the mattress in an effort to get away from me. I wasn't sure I believed him, but I reached in and removed the socks from his mouth. He started panting wildly. "What the fuck? What are you doing? Untie me!"

I pretended to consider the request for a few seconds before shaking my head. "I can't do that. You said you wanted to come here and play with me, so let's play." I fixed him with the same look I'd given in the living room when I had knelt at his feet with wide, innocent eyes and a blow-job-lips pout. "I even got us some toys," I added, gesturing to the tools out of reach to his left.

Bruce looked down in horror at the screwdriver still sticking out of his ribs. He couldn't reach for it with his wrists bound behind his back. "Are you insane? Look what you did! Pull it out! Pull it out!"

"If you insist." I yanked it out by the handle. He grunted painfully but didn't scream. The trickle of blood turned to a stream.

"You have to take me to the hospital!" He started breathing more quickly and I wondered if he might start to hyperventilate.

"Come on, Bruce," I said, tenderly stroking the side of his face. "I chose you because I thought you were smarter than that. You must realize by now that no one's going to the hospital. Now, do you want another drink? It'll help with the pain."

He kept panting and wheezing and staring at his wound. I held the glass of murky liquid under his nose, pressing it to his lips. He took a few gulps, then filled up his mouth and spat into my face. Cold alcohol and juice splashed into my eyes and up my nose. A clinical, medicinal smell clogged my nostrils. I sputtered, momentarily stunned, then used the blousy top of my dress to dry my face. He didn't take advantage of my distraction by trying to escape. It seemed this would be his one and only rebellious act of the night.

"Okay, so, your drinking privileges are now revoked, and I'm putting the gag back in." Before he could protest, I shoved the thick socks into his mouth once again. "You have no idea how stupid that was."

Staring at his face, I could almost watch his skin turning paler shade by shade as he lost blood. The blush I had seen the first time we met was gone, possibly for good, and his freckles stood out prominently. He tried to scream around the socks, but the sound was muffled and useless.

I grabbed a handful of individual razor blades and straddled his lap the way I had on the couch. I made the corner of one bite into his flesh. I embedded it until half the razor had disappeared inside him. His skin yielded as if it were modeling clay. I drove four more little blades into his chest in a straight line. He screamed until his voice went hoarse, the sound almost completely stopped by the socks, and then he made sounds that were supposed to be screams but came out as defeated, impotent rasps.

"It's kinda like when you scream in a dream, isn't it?" I asked him. "You want to make sounds so badly, but it's just a whisper."

I watched his dark brown eyes as they stared at me in terror and pain. They reminded me of the beady eyes of all the squirrels I had tortured with push pins and rusty blades. I'd wanted to kill a human because they must be different from the tiny creatures that were so easy to catch. Human prey, I had always thought, would be more challenging and well worth the extra work. But right now, the only differences I saw between him and them were the much more involved cleanup and the overwhelming probability that no one had ever gone to prison for slicing up a garden pest or two.

I lightly touched the dull sides of the razor blades sticking out of his chest with one gentle fingertip. With every movement, Bruce twitched in discomfort.

"I could make you into a porcupine with razors for spines," I said dreamily. He tried to scream again.

The door opened a few inches and Robin tentatively stepped through. When Bruce saw her, he started grunting and pleading with his eyes for her to save him. Robin studiously avoided eye contact with him, instead focusing on me. I smiled wide and gestured for her to come sit next to me.

CHAPTER 14

Robin

February 2008

I did what she asked, crossing the room and sitting next to her on the plastic-covered carpet to face the naked, restrained boy head-on. Allegra strummed the half-exposed razor blades in his chest like a child's toy guitar strings, trying to decide what to do next. It took me a few seconds to register how deeply she had embedded them.

Her face suddenly lit up. "I have a great idea. Be right back." She scrambled to a standing position and skipped out the door, leaving me alone on the floor with Bruce.

Sweat beaded on his forehead. His bare chest heaved as he tried to inhale through the gag, the tiny blades rising and falling. His eyes were perfect circles, pupils large and shiny in the dim room. I stared at him, and he panted in my general direction. My gaze landed on a circular wound in his stomach, a thin but steady stream of blood oozing from it.

"Oh, shit," I said quietly.

Without thinking, I snatched the gag out of his mouth, pressing the slimy wad covered with spit and regurgitated bile against the wound to try and staunch the flow. Bruce took a huge breath through his mouth, and then started sobbing and panting.

"Who the fuck are you? Who the fuck is *she*? What the fuck is going on here? What does she want from me? Jesus, why did I come here? Can you help me get out? I need to go to the fucking hospital! Look at my fucking stomach!"

Tiny red droplets had started accumulating around the razor blades in his chest. The stream of blood from his stomach continued, turning the faded lime green color of the socks to a sickly brown as it mixed with his other fluids. When he opened his mouth to scream at me again, I noticed a pink sheen on his front teeth.

A faint ringing echoed in my ears, and my entire body started buzzing. Images of jagged broken bones and internal bleeding filled my head and prevented me from thinking of anything else. What the hell was taking Allegra so long?

"Can you please shut up?" I asked him quietly. I removed the socks from his stomach and my eyes immediately fixated on the wound again, the raw red of the perfectly circular hole and pasty white skin beyond. I realized covering it had been more for me than him. The stream had finally thinned, and I wondered if that was because of my assistance with the slobbery socks or because his body was running out of blood. Maybe both.

"No! Fuck you! Is this what you sick fucks do? Does it make you feel better about your own stupid, shitty life that you have to kill a random guy? What the fuck is wrong with you? How many people have you killed?!"

I dropped the socks to the plastic floor and continued staring at his abdomen. At the damage I had helped Allegra cause.

"Huh? Answer me, you bitch! How many people have you killed?!"

I swear to whatever's watching us from the sky that I had no conscious control over what happened next. I pinched one of the blades between my thumb and index finger and wrenched it out of his chest with a grunt. He was so surprised by my sudden movement that he didn't make a sound as I slashed a hard vertical line down his throat parallel to his Adam's apple.

He had been in the middle of saying, "Go fuck yourself, you crazy who—"

Halfway through the last word in his sentence, his voice became a rough gurgle. After what seemed like a full thirty seconds at least, the line thickened until dark red blood spilled over and covered his chest. The effect was an ombre pattern that started out magenta and thinned into unpredictable pink lines traveling down his torso. They became dark again as the liquid pooled in his lap until his wrinkled balls and flaccid penis were completely submerged. Once again, I couldn't stop staring at the damage I had caused.

The bedroom door opened and Allegra bounded back in with a clear glass jar in hand, wearing the scarf I made her. I watched her face as she tried to decide whether she was angry that I had slashed the guy without her or proud of my initiative. She decided on the latter and kept the grin she had come in with.

"Wow," she said with a giggle, "there's a lot more blood in here now than there was when I left."

Bruce gurgled again and the stream of blood coming from his neck intensified so much that I wondered if I'd hit an artery. His face was whiter than I thought faces could get. He was no longer able to focus his eyes. Wet red from his lap seeped under his knobby knees and soaked into the black jeans I would now need to get rid of.

Allegra straddled Bruce's lap and set the jar down beside him. She completely ignored the blood everywhere, even when his hand spasmed involuntarily and sent a small wave splashing against her bare thigh. The end of the gray scarf landed directly in Bruce's lap and started soaking up blood from the accumulated puddle. She slapped his face a few times until he appeared to look back at her.

"Hey," she said loudly. "Hey man, no going unconscious yet. We're not done with you."

He coughed. The pink sheen on his teeth had turned to an unmistakable red.

She turned sideways and looked at me. "Can I use that razor?" she asked, and I realized I was still holding the small blade I had cut his throat with. When I handed it over, a viscous rope of partially congealed blood stretched between it and my fingers and hers until it was severed by distance.

"Bruce!" Allegra said loudly, trying to reach him through his stupor of alcohol and blood loss. "Bruce, this is really cool. I want to show you something."

When she was satisfied that Bruce was looking at her, Allegra pinched one of his eyelids with one hand and raised the sticky blade with the other. In one fluid motion, she sliced off his eyelid, dangled the gummy shred of flesh in front of his face for a few seconds, and then dropped it into the jar next to her. The clear liquid looked like water, but as soon as I saw tiny reactive bubbles, I realized it must have been some of the lye solution she had made that morning. The contents turned a reddish brown as she casually swirled them like a glass of wine. She held the jar in front of his face, ignoring his renewed attempts to scream past his slashed throat.

"Look," she said over his rasping. "This is what's gonna happen to your whole body. In my bathtub. You'll just… Dissolve."

He gave a low moan, then exploded in an involuntary sputtering cough that left Allegra's face and cleavage splatter-painted red. Without a word, she stood up, retrieved the discolored socks from the floor, and shoved them into his mouth so hard they probably ended up halfway down his throat. The fabric must have cut off his air supply or something because he was permanently unconscious less than a minute later.

"No! Fuck!" Allegra let out an animalistic shriek and kicked Bruce's shoulder. The body tipped over and made an inappropriately comical splash in the inches of blood pooled on the plastic tarp. I winced at the wet thud and started sidestepping toward the door without turning my back on either of them.

"I can't believe it's over already," Allegra said to the blood puddles. She was no longer the sexy, confident schemer that she had been when Bruce was alive. Now she had nothing to look forward to, only a huge task with a ticking clock before someone smelled something and called the apartment complex's front office. She kneeled next to Bruce's head and examined what she'd done to his eyelid, staining her bare knees red.

I finally made it to the door and opened it, casting a triangle of yellow light onto all that reflective plastic. She finally looked at me when she noticed the movement.

"Where are you going?" Allegra asked me.

"To take a shower," I answered numbly.

"I love you."

"Yeah," I said as I stepped through the door. "Love you, too." I couldn't believe it, but even after what I'd just seen, this was still true.

Hours later, in what my dad used to call the tiny hours of the morning, Allegra finally slunk into my room wearing a clean white t-shirt and black underwear. I did a double-take to confirm that her hair wasn't still ropy with blood and sweat, but it was just damp from the shower. She knew I was awake even though my eyes were closed against the gentle glow of the TV. Without a word, she climbed into bed and snuggled under my outstretched arm. When she kissed the side of my neck, a not-so-subtle way of seeing whether I was awake enough to fool around, I didn't open my eyes.

The next morning, I woke up before Allegra and moved to the living room to knit and listen to music. When I walked past the second bedroom, I got the feeling of a presence behind the door. I shuddered involuntarily and tried to convince myself it was because the AC in the apartment was lower than usual to preserve Bruce until he could be disposed of. I debated opening the door for about two milliseconds, then continued down the hallway to the kitchen to make coffee.

I was supposed to have the day off, but someone always called out on Saturdays. When the music playing on my phone stopped abruptly to let through a phone call from my boss asking me to cover a six-hour shift, I decided to take it. I had been planning to help Allegra clean up the crime scene today, but since the thought of trying to pick up the plastic tarp without any day-old gore spilling onto the carpet made me sick, this would be a good excuse.

When I went to my bedroom and got dressed for work, Allegra wasn't there. I walked back to the murder room door, which was now ajar. I found her surveying the gruesome scene in her shirt from last night, a pair of my pajama pants, and the gray scarf I had made for her, the blood stain now more brown than red.

The whole scene was much worse now that it had been sitting for six hours. It didn't look like she'd done much in the way of cleanup after I'd left the night before, but one of his legs was missing most of the skin between the knee and ankle which told me that maybe she had been experimenting with the hacksaw. Bruce's body was an island in a sea of his own blood, but now that blood had a congealed brownish film over the top, like stagnant heated milk. The room stunk of putrid excrement and sweet rotting meat, amplified by the cold instead of reduced by it. His face was frozen in a joyless, unnatural grimace, his deformed eye wide open and sightless. The side of his body closest to the floor was purple from gravity collecting anything left inside him and pushing it to the lowest point. The skin on his stomach looked puffy and pink around the circular wound that was now just a black hole the size of my thumbnail. Every color was as vibrant as it was horrifying. Looking at him hurt my eyes the same way it hurts to look at the sun.

Allegra had waded through the blood in her bare feet and now stood staring at the body with gore creeping up the plaid hem of my pants. She seemed at a loss for what to do next. She bent down and removed a red plastic bracelet from his wrist and put it on her own before noticing I was watching from the doorway.

"I wanted something to remember this by," she told me unapologetically.

"I didn't say anything," I responded.

She looked at my all-black clothes, including different black jeans from the ones ruined the previous night, and the green apron slung over my shoulder.

"You going to work? I thought you were off today."

"Yeah, someone called out. I'll be home around five."

She nodded and went back to examining her project.

Over the next week, I was a fly on the wall as Ally slowly disposed of Bruce's body. I think it was a lot more work than she had anticipated. The sound of her lightweight tools sawing and chiseling through bone haunted me when I was home. The smell got worse by the hour. Even though more of Bruce was fed into the horrifying soup in our bathtub every day, the smell of rotten steak, dirty diapers, and decayed garbage seemed to increase rather than dissipate.

Allegra didn't go to school or leave the apartment at all. She didn't even shower elsewhere, claiming a shower would be her reward once she was all done. She spent most of her time hacking away at Bruce's body parts until they were in small enough pieces to be dropped into the tub. She had done enough research to know that the lye solution wouldn't destroy the bathtub, but not enough to realize how toxic the air would become without something to seal the tub shut. We kept the door to the bathroom closed at all times and stuffed towels into the gap underneath. I detoured to the store after work on day two, coming home with two N95 respirator masks and a pair of thick rubber gloves for Ally. I found that a spritz of perfume inside my mask made the smell bearable. The apartment was still freezing, and she still wore that stupid gray scarf with the brown stain on the edge every day. I took to sleeping in leggings and a sweatshirt, wrapped in a cocoon of blankets. Around the fourth night, she stopped trying to crawl in and join me.

The bathroom became Allegra's laboratory. When the river of blood and most of the plastic had disappeared, she moved the remaining pieces of Bruce onto a clean tarp on the bathroom floor. Even though the head had been one of the first sections to go, this was exactly as creepy as it sounds. I only peed at home in emergencies, saving all other bathroom activity until I got to work. On day five, I went to my dad's house to shower, giving the excuse of a broken fixture that the landlord needed to order parts to fix. Dad offered to give it a shot since landlords can be unreliable or shifty, but I nervously declined.

Day nine was a rare Sunday that I wasn't scheduled to work. The curtain was already pulled back, sunlight brightening every inch of the bedroom, when I woke up. I detangled from my nest of blankets and padded into the hallway in my socks. In the hallway, I noticed the scent of coffee and bread instead of rotten flesh and chemicals. The living room and kitchen were as bright as the bedroom, more morning sun spilling in from the glass patio door. Allegra stood in the kitchen, hunched and peering into the oven.

"Are you…cooking?" I asked.

She turned to face me, an easy smile on her face. "It's just biscuits out of a tube, but yeah. I wanted to do something nice."

I took the steaming mug she handed me and absentmindedly took a sip. It was doctored exactly the way I liked it. I frowned at the cup.

"What's wrong?" she asked.

"Well, first of all, there are body parts in my bathroom…" At some point in the last few days, in an effort to make it more palatable, I had started joking about the little apocalypse currently booming in our universe.

"Not anymore!" Ally bounced on her heels with excitement, the ends of her hair swaying elegantly. "I checked this morning, and the rest of him is officially gone! All I have to do now is get rid of the liquid, but that'll be easy."

"Wait, really?"

I power-walked to the bathroom and opened the door. Sure enough, the only thing amiss was a covered industrial bucket half-hidden between the tub and toilet. The smell of decay was a little stronger here, but there was also a sharp aroma of bleach and cleaning products in the air. All the white surfaces in the bathroom were sparkling, including the interior of the bathtub.

Allegra came up behind me in the bathroom doorway. "Pretty good, right?"

I nodded. "Yup, pretty good."

I walked past her and looked into the second bedroom's open door. Incredibly, it looked the same as it had before we met Bruce. Dresser, lamp, bare mattress, and unblemished carpet. When I turned to face Allegra, she brought her face close to mine and tried to kiss me. I backed away and inhaled deeply.

"It looks back to normal," I said.

"Exactly, and now we can get back to normal too!"

"What do you mean?" I took a couple of steps back, retreating to my bedroom doorway.

"Well, I know you haven't exactly been loving the stuff going on around here this week. Now we can go back to how it was before."

I didn't know what to say. I could barely remember how "before" had even felt. "I can't picture what that looks like."

She laughed like I told a hilarious joke and started to follow me into my room. I blocked her from entering.

"I'm serious, Ally. We never talked about after. How do you really picture our life now? I just keep going to work? You flirt your way back into school and keep choreographing for the dance team? In two weeks, or six months, or whenever you get bored, we just go get another homeless kid and do this all over again?"

"I hadn't thought about it, but... Yeah, basically. Why not?"

I couldn't tell if she was really confused about why this wasn't a feasible life plan. If her furrowed brow and pouty lips were just for show, she was a great actress. I allowed my eyes to focus on a spot on the carpet instead of her face.

"I want to be by myself," I said quietly. "I need to think about all of this. I just...don't want you in my room anymore."

"Well then where the hell am I supposed to sleep?" she asked, dumbfounded.

Her inability to grasp what I was saying triggered a flash of annoyance. I couldn't help the harshness in my voice or the aggression of my movements. "*Your* room." I gestured sharply to the murder room with one hand.

Wordless except for some profanities muttered under her breath, Allegra took the mug of coffee out of my hands and returned to the kitchen. She poured it down the sink, then grabbed the pot and emptied it into the sink as well.

"Thanks for being so mature about this," I told her sarcastically. She flipped me off. I retreated to *my* room and locked the door from the inside.

PART THREE

CHAPTER 15

Allegra

March-April 2008

The day before Toby's fourteenth birthday, Mom called and invited Robin and me to celebrate with a lunch at their house. I agreed for both of us, even though I had no idea whether Robin would want to be in the same room with me long enough to sing Happy Birthday to my brother. Within three weeks, we had gone from inseparable to strangers, grunting in passing about groceries that needed to be bought or a carpet stain that needed to be cleaned.

I'd dropped out of community college, so my only responsibility was showing up to Andrea's classroom every Monday. Otherwise, I stayed in my room drinking cheap wine from the gas station that didn't check IDs. Robin went to work, came home, and sequestered herself in her room until morning. I heard the TV going at all hours of the night, meaning she had probably returned to her insomniac ways. Night felt so empty with her and the screen in another room.

I knew Robin was still upset by everything that had happened with Bruce. I don't think she'd expected to be so incredibly involved in the murder itself. I certainly hadn't expected it, so when I came back into the room and found that she had slit his throat wide open, it thrilled me in a way I wasn't ready for. It felt like the beginning of an era where we would kill together—instead of the beginning of the end of our relationship.

I hung up with my mom and checked the time on my cell phone: 6:07 p.m. The front door of the apartment unlocked, opened, closed, and locked. Robin's purse jingled to the floor, followed by the thump-thump of her shoes.

"Hi!" I called through the open door of *my* room, where I lie diagonally across the made bed in a black sports bra and matching Soffe shorts. There was no answer.

A few seconds later, Robin padded down the carpeted hallway in her socks, the white cord from her earbuds stark against her all-black uniform. I waved, and she bent her elbow slightly and wiggled a few fingers in acknowledgment before disappearing behind her door.

"Oh, for god's sake, this is ridiculous," I muttered under my breath. The clicking of her latch brought the last three weeks of her ignoring and dismissing me flooding back, and suddenly I was finished with whatever her stupid game was. I rolled off the bed and stormed across the hall and into *her* room without knocking.

Robin stood in the middle of the room, staring at the TV with her shirt pulled halfway over her torso. She snapped out of her trance when I entered the room. She wasn't wearing the iPod anymore, so she had no excuse not to hear me. She hurried to cover her bra and stomach as if I hadn't seen her naked a million times.

"My mom invited us to their house for Toby's birthday tomorrow. Wanna go?" I asked as if everything were normal between us.

Robin stared at me almost as blankly as she had just been staring at the TV screen. Her eyes narrowed slowly, shifting her expression to one of absolute incredulity.

"No," she said, a loaded syllable that implied I was the dumbest person on the planet.

"Okay, fine, just asking." I shrugged and started to leave the room.

"You really have some nerve, Allegra." Her voice was much stronger when she spoke to the back of my head.

I whipped around to face her again, my ponytail smacking against the door in the process. "*I* have some nerve?"

"Yeah, coming in here all casual and asking if I want to come to your parents' house for lunch? Like nothing happened, after all the shit that went down in this apartment? After what we *did*?"

My eyes narrowed and my breath became shallow. "Hey, I told you from the beginning what I wanted to do. No one forced you to help."

She crossed her arms across her chest and shifted her gaze away from me. "You knew I didn't want to."

"But you did."

"But I didn't *want* to!"

"But… You *did*! I can argue this very simple point for hours, Robin! What do you want from me?" I flung my hands out in a dramatic gesture to emphasize my last point and hit my ring and pinky knuckles hard against the door frame. The loud knock and resulting sting made me curse loudly. I couldn't be sure, but it looked like Robin was holding in a smirk at my pain.

"Nothing," she said measuredly. "I don't want anything from you. I especially don't want to go to your fucking family's house for lunch and pretend that we're… Anything. Anymore."

I wasn't worried that she actually meant it. There was no way Robin would leave me now that Bruce was our mutual secret. As I left Robin's room and wandered back to my own, Bruce's bracelet glimmered briefly on my wrist, catching my eye. It was a thick piece of white elastic with a collection of unique red plastic beads arranged in no particular pattern, probably something he had impulsively shoved into his pocket at the dollar store, but it didn't matter that the trophy was cheap and forgettable. It simply mattered that I had a trophy. I was the only one who needed to know its significance.

Lunch at my parents' house was as ordinary as it could possibly have been. They greeted me at the front door and offered me a drink like I was company and not their daughter who had moved out less than a year ago. The bathroom had also been scrubbed and polished to a degree usually only reserved for guests. Dad grilled hotdogs and burgers, per Toby's request, and had commissioned the doughnut shop to make a multi-layered doughnut cake with traditional glaze, chocolate sprinkles, and fourteen glistening black candles stuck haphazardly into a row of doughnut holes on top. Doughnut cakes were a tradition in our family because of where Dad worked, so Toby must have been expecting it, but he still looked excited when Mom brought the cake out. I didn't tell him the chocolate sprinkles looked like little ants crawling all over the sugary treat. When Toby blew out the candles, it occurred to me just how idyllic the day was. Not that our parents usually locked us in cages and forced us to eat gruel, but there was a feeling of ease in the house that I didn't remember from when I lived there. Everyone was happy and interaction didn't feel forced.

After the candles were blown out, my mom instructed Toby and me to sit down in the living room and she would bring our doughnuts to us along with his presents. The moment she said "presents," I realized I didn't bring one. I tried to think of something that would have been back-ordered so I could at least give Toby a verbal IOU, but came up blank. I studied my brother, one leg up on the arm of the couch, engrossed in his handheld video game. His black jeans had faded to gray and the bottoms were torn to shreds from him constantly walking on them. I'd seen him in that stupid Freddy Krueger t-shirt a million times and it was starting to develop holes from over-wear. Then it came to me: the perfect experience-based present.

As my parents carried in doughnuts on paper plates and a few brightly wrapped boxes, I straightened my spine and raised my eyebrows in Toby's direction, morphing into Good Big Sister mode.

"Hey, Toby, wanna know what I got you?"

"I guess," he says, not looking up from his game.

"It's not something you can open today…" I started.

He abruptly cut me off without waiting for the second half of my sentence. "Then what's the point?"

"The point is getting you some cool new clothes. I want to take you shopping." My smile made my jaw ache but I kept it pasted on.

"Wow, Allegra, that's a great idea!" my mom exclaimed as she handed me my plate and dropped onto the couch. "He wouldn't even let me take him school shopping at the beginning of the year."

"That's because the stores you like are gross!" Toby exploded in a fit of teenage angst. "None of my friends wear clothes from department stores, those are for preppy losers."

Dad handed Toby his plate and sat next to him on the couch. Toby kept his scowl even as he picked up the sticky doughnut with his fingers and took a giant bite. His cheeks expanded like a chipmunk's as he chewed.

"What about Hot Topic, then?" I asked.

Toby's face lit up for about one second before he remembered that cool kids don't do that. "That could work," he said pseudo-nonchalantly. He shot a glance at Mom and added, "Sully's parents let *him* wear stuff from Hot Topic." I assumed Sully was one of his friends from the movie club, if they were even still doing that.

"Toby, I never said you can't wear clothes from Hot Topic. It's just that going in there freaks me out. I'm glad your sister wants to take you."

"Yeah," Dad inserted. "You can come back with one of those chains on your pants, some guyliner, and a mohawk!"

Mom shot Dad a glare, but her face softened after a few seconds because of Dad's huge, troublemaking grin. Even Toby cracked another smile at Dad's goofiness.

"I don't even want to be that extreme," Toby said. "I just don't wanna look like some preppy loser wannabe. Maybe like… I don't know, some cool jewelry or something, maybe a studded belt. Your bracelets are cool, maybe something like those. Where'd you get them?" He pointed at my left wrist where Bruce's red beaded bracelet sat inconspicuously among three others.

My stomach dropped. I lowered my gaze so my family wouldn't see how caught off guard I was by this simple question. The absolute last thing I expected today was for someone to bring attention to my first piece of murder memorabilia. I played with the bracelets with my right hand for a few seconds, pretending to try to remember where I got them.

"I don't remember. Here and there," I answered, shrugging. "They didn't all come in a pack or anything. But I'm sure Hot Topic has something similar."

I looked up at Mom, who was still staring at my left wrist even though Dad and Toby had continued the conversation. When she noticed me looking, she shook her head almost imperceptibly and then slipped the hostess smile seamlessly back onto her face.

"Toby, why don't you open your presents?" she asked, handing him one of the packages. "This one is from Aunt Carol and Uncle Bob, but they asked me to wrap it for them so the wrapping didn't get ruined in the mail."

Toby became immediately distracted by his gifts, and Mom and Dad got caught up with taking pictures for our extended family so they could see Toby opening the gifts they sent. He received a lot of clothes, mostly jeans and t-shirts, a couple CDs, and an enormous coffee-table book about the making of classic horror movies. Mom and Dad got him a few video games and a beanie with a picture of the *IT* clown on one side, and the words 'You'll Float Too' in a creepy font on the other. After the fifth or sixth item on the same theme, I started to wonder if always getting presents based on your only interest was annoying or awesome.

After Toby finished opening his final gift, Mom offered everyone another doughnut. I declined, saying I should probably get home, even though Robin hated me and I had nothing to do there. Toby and I started walking to the downstairs bathroom at the same time, but he got there a split second before me and touched the doorknob first, which meant I was stuck climbing the stairs to use the master bathroom connected to our parents' room.

Before entering the bathroom, I snooped in a couple of dresser drawers, the trash can in the corner, and both closets in Mom and Dad's bedroom. Same old clothes, earrings, books, garbage. I wanted the same thrill that secretly looking through their stuff had given me when I lived here, but I didn't really care about the finer points of my family's lives now that they didn't directly affect mine.

I stepped onto the white tile of my parents' bathroom and opened the medicine cabinet absentmindedly. Everything inside was also painfully ordinary: tweezers, nail clippers, Q-tips, tubes of ointment, adhesive bandages, and five or six orange prescription bottles that all had my mom's name on them. Now *that* piqued my interest; I hadn't known my mom was on any medication, let alone a handful a day. I recognized a couple of the names as anti-anxiety pills that high school acquaintances had told me they'd tried, never in the context of diagnosed anxiety. The most interesting name was quetiapine, identified in fine print with the brand name Seroquel.

I put the bottle back into the cabinet and made sure everything inside looked like it had when I opened it. As I sat on the toilet, I searched 'quetiapine' on the smartphone I'd gotten just a couple months earlier. It didn't take long to figure out that it was a pill used to treat bipolar disorder, schizophrenia, and severe depression. I pulled up my pants, flushed the toilet, and stole a single pill from the quetiapine bottle on my way out. The pill was round and white with a few numbers etched onto one side.

Coming downstairs, the first room to the left was the kitchen. As I walked down the final few steps, I heard my parents arguing in the kitchen. They were yell-whispering intensely, probably because they didn't want us to hear, which, of course, made me want to hear even more. I recognized the tone as one that I had heard late at night as a kid when I was supposed to be in bed and the grownups needed to have a *serious discussion.*

"No, I'm one hundred percent sure," my mom whispered.

"How can you possibly be? It's a beaded bracelet, Babe. There are literally millions of them, more made every day."

My dad didn't sound concerned, but I instantly realized what Mom was upset about. I pressed my back against the wall next to the kitchen doorway so they wouldn't see me if they glanced in my direction.

"I swear to God it's the one he made. I don't know why she would have it, but I know it is. I was there! I helped him work out the pattern!"

"Okay, it's okay. Maybe it is his… But how would Allegra have even gotten it? Didn't you tell me the bead workshop happened *after* she visited Foundation House?"

"Yes! That's why I'm so fucking weirded out, Michael! I don't know what her connection with him is, but they must have one. He's been missing for weeks and now she shows up wearing a one-of-a-kind bracelet that I. Saw. Him. Make?" Somehow, even though she was still whispering, I could tell the register of her voice was rising as she became more upset. "Maybe she knows where he went. I should go ask her."

"Do you want to go lie down for a while?" Dad asked in his normal speaking voice. "Maybe take something to help you calm down? I know this kid's disappearance has been hard on you, but how many times have you told me you can never count on these kids for anything? It sounds like this one, in particular, is pretty transient. I bet he'll show up soon so you can yell at him for how worried he's made you."

Mom sighed forcefully and then took a long, slow breath in. "You're probably right. He's just never gone this long without checking in…"

Her voice faded as I walked out of earshot of their quiet conversation.

"Bye, Toby. Happy birthday," I said quickly as I gathered my purse from the living room couch.

"Yeah, bye," Toby said, engrossed in his game again.

"Bye, guys!" I called to my parents. I heard movement from the kitchen, but I was out the front door before they had time to come all the way out.

I chastised myself all the way home on the bus. How could I have been so stupid as to wear Bruce's bracelet around Mom? I mean, I had no way of knowing she would recognize it, but I should have considered his connection to her. I had forgotten how much Mom actually cared about all her kids at Foundation House. Furthermore, I'd never realized how observant she was of tiny details like the bead pattern. I would never have been caught dead doing something as stupid as a beading workshop, but even if it were my thing, I don't think the exact pattern I chose would have stuck with me the way it obviously stuck with her.

And speaking of things I didn't know about Mom, I'd been snooping in her stuff for years. I had read mail that was none of my business, poked through her dresser drawers, and opened every box and bag in her closet. How had I never noticed the prescription bottles before? If she had a serious mental illness like the ones those pills treated, why didn't I know about it?

I took the pill out of my pocket and examined it, pinching it tightly between my thumb and index so I wouldn't drop it on the floor of the bus. Aside from the tiny numbers, which I assumed were specific to this particular medication, it looked like every single white pill I'd ever seen.

It looked like the over-the-counter painkillers that Robin and I kept around for headaches. How important was this pill to my mother's daily functioning? If I switched the prescription from Mom's cabinet with the generic painkillers in my own, what would happen? Would she be too distracted by mystery symptoms to remember I'm wearing her missing kid's bracelet?

"Excuse me," a deep voice said to my right.

I startled and stuffed the pill back into the pocket of my jeans. A vaguely attractive man in his mid-thirties, clear brown skin shining with a layer of sweat and glasses glinting in the sunlight, stood in the aisle eyeing the seat next to me. He swiped his brunette hair out of his eyes.

"Hi," he said when I was looking at him. "Is that seat taken?"

I was in a window seat in the third row of the bus. I looked at the empty aisle seat next to me, then glanced pointedly at the rest of the bus, which was almost empty. Besides me and the guy, the only other passengers were a group of middle schoolers at the back.

"Yes," I said. I resumed staring straight ahead and hoped he would go away.

The guy smiled, revealing teeth that were perfectly white but quite crooked. "Are you sure? Looks like you're riding alone. Mind if I sit with you?"

"Oh my god," I said, shifting my gaze back to him. "There are like forty other seats in here. I'm not in the mood for this today. Can you go away please?"

He put his hands up in a "whoa, there" gesture. As he retreated to another row, I heard him mutter something about "just trying to talk to" me. *Exactly,* I wanted to say, *and I don't want to be fucking talked to.* But that would only have invited more conversation.

I realized we were already approaching the closest stop to my apartment and pulled the yellow cord above my head. The driver pulled to a stop and actually tipped his hat to me on my way down the stairs.

I was still smirking about the hat-tip when I unlocked the door and stepped into our living room. To my surprise, Robin was sitting on the living room couch knitting and listening to something on her iPod. She didn't say anything, but she waved and pursed her lips into an expression that I chose to interpret as a smile. I also chose to interpret it as the first step to her loving me again. I knew she wouldn't freeze me out forever.

•——

Switching my mom's pills was so easy that it didn't even feel like an accomplishment. In the weeks between Toby's birthday and Easter, I decided that making the switch was necessary to curb her suspicion that my bracelet was the same one she had seen Bruce make. If taking away her medication didn't immediately send her into some kind of psychotic episode, she would probably have withdrawal symptoms distracting enough that she wouldn't have time to wonder about Bruce's disappearance at all. By the time she called her doctor and got new pills, she would have forgotten all about the bracelet. I would just never wear it around her again.

Robin and I were invited to my parents' house for Easter Sunday, but she opted to go to work and make time-and-a-half serving lattes and frappuccinos. I was pretty sure that she would have otherwise said yes, since the figurative layer of ice that had permeated our apartment after I finished getting rid of Bruce had recently started to thaw as she came to terms with what we did. She actually spoke to me in full sentences and greeted me when she got home from work now. She had also started spending more time in common areas like the living room and kitchen. I hadn't been invited back to her room yet, but it was probably only a matter of time.

I timed the switch perfectly. When we were done eating ham and twice-baked potatoes, Toby stood up and headed toward the downstairs bathroom. I followed and re-created the moment on his birthday when he got there a few seconds before me, forcing me to go upstairs. Once in my parents' bathroom, I emptied my mom's prescription bottle of quetiapine into my palm and counted twenty-two pills. Just as I thought, a handful of these looked identical to the handful of pain relievers I had stuck in my hoodie pocket before leaving my apartment.

I came back downstairs to Toby hooking up the living room TV to a video camera he had borrowed from school. He wanted to show us a short film his horror club had been working on, which he swore was only twenty minutes long, so I agreed to stay and watch. The film itself was only twenty minutes long, but he failed to mention all the behind-the-scenes shots and bloopers that we just *had* to see because they were *so* cool and funny. By the time we had seen all the footage, the few buses that ran on Easter Sunday had made their final stops, and Dad offered to drive me home.

I stepped out of the car in the parking lot of my apartment complex, the twenty-two quetiapine knocking together quietly in my pocket.

"Bye, Dad. Thanks for the ride," I said. The pink and orange desert sunset was barely visible behind the tan buildings. The car cast a light shadow on the darkening asphalt.

"You bet, Al. Love you!"

I slammed the car door, and he waved on his way out of the complex.

When I got to my room, I dumped the pills onto my bed and looked at them again. Before I could talk myself out of it, I picked up two and swallowed them dry. Then I put the rest into the empty acetaminophen bottle in the bathroom and waited in the living room for Robin to get home.

"Hey, stranger," I greeted her when she unlocked the door forty-five minutes later.

"Uh… Hey." She kicked off her shoes and dropped her purse to the floor. She was also carrying a brown paper bag with that famous green mermaid on the side. Holding it up, she said, "I was on fridge clean-out duty today. Free pastries that expire at midnight."

"Oohhh!" I exclaimed, clapping my hands excitedly.

She set the bag down on the kitchen counter and studied me for a few seconds. "Been drinking?"

"No," I replied, smiling secretively. "I…am high. And you…"

"Have to babysit you all night? Awesome, thanks for that. What are you on?"

"No, silly. I was going to say, you should be high too."

Robin laughed sarcastically. "Sure, I can definitely see that happening."

I groaned loudly. "You're so much meaner to me now!" She didn't say anything. "I just took a couple of my mom's pills. The rest are in the bathroom. Go have some."

She disappeared into the bathroom, emerging a few seconds or minutes later with the white acetaminophen bottle. "These? Oh shit, you actually switched them? I didn't think you were serious. Thanks for telling me before I got a headache anyway."

I smirked because she had underestimated me, and I had overperformed. "Seriously… I just feel super mellow and light. No thoughts in my head. It's nice."

I could tell she was considering it. She opened the bottle and peered inside, then shook a single pill into her palm. "It's not poison or something, is it?"

"Holy shit, no! Why would I poison you?"

She snapped her head up and shot me a glare.

"Robin." I stood up and walked over to her. "I will never do anything to hurt you. I just want you to feel better. It'll help, okay? I promise."

She stared at my face for a few more seconds, her features softening as she considered. Then she shrugged and tossed the single pill into her mouth.

"Fuck it," she said, swallowing.

"Yeah! Fuck it! Okay!" I took the bottle out of her hands and replaced the lid. "I'll go put this away. Then we can— Can I watch TV with you?"

I left to replace the pills and give her time to consider letting me back into her room. When I got back to the living room, she wasn't there and the paper bag was gone.

"You coming?" Robin called. I approached her bedroom door and opened it. Inside, her pink lamp glowed warmly and the TV was tuned to a sitcom rerun. She leaned against the pillows with the bag of pastries in her lap. The hat she was currently knitting was next to her on the blanket. She had left me a spot.

"Were there any chocolate croissants today?" I asked, approaching the bed cautiously.

She pulled two out of the bag and handed them to me along with a few napkins. "Of course. Don't get crumbs in my bed." We laughed lightly together.

A few episodes later, we were both encased in a cocoon of tingly, lightheaded warmth. At some point, we had each taken one more pill, and an hour later agreed that that had been an excellent idea. I'd started out the night in jeans, a hoodie, and a pink patterned T-shirt, but had overheated and stripped down to just the shirt and my bikini-style undies. Robin had changed out of her work clothes into pajama pants and a tank top during a commercial break. She turned off the lamp before coming back to bed. We took turns sinking into the pillows and dozing until the early morning.

I opened my eyes in the dark and saw that Robin was awake, too.

"What happened to us?" I whispered to her.

She blinked slowly. "We killed a guy," she answered sleepily.

"And now you hate me."

"I hate…myself. For getting involved."

"But you don't hate me?" I smiled hopefully.

She scoffed. "No, Allegra, I don't *hate* you. I just needed some time to process all this."

"*Needed?* Past tense?"

Robin rolled onto her side, facing away from me, and scooted a few inches backward until we were spooning. Once I realized she was actually initiating contact with me, I put my arm around her and nestled my face into her messy mop of hair. I realized she had fallen asleep without answering my question and allowed her deep, steady breathing to lull me back under my own blanket of unconsciousness.

CHAPTER 16

Robin

April 2008

The apartment is dark and cold. Even the carpet feels frigid under my bare feet, like frosted grass in winter. I pad down the hallway, reaching for the wall on either side. The walls are farther apart than I remember; with my arms fully extended, my fingertips just barely brush them. I'm aware of a rectangle of light in my peripheral vision, and when I turn toward it, I realize it is the doorway to Allegra's bedroom.

I approach the door and push it open, revealing the brightest overhead lights I've ever seen. Everything in the room is illuminated with harsh white light. Allegra kneels next to Bruce's body, which is propped against the mattress in a sitting position. She studiously drives a screwdriver into his abdomen over and over again, puncturing him with perfectly circular holes. Instead of bleeding, the holes gently ooze a dark, rancid liquid that I can smell from the doorway. He isn't making any noise. His eyes are glazed and his lips are blue. Allegra doesn't realize he's already dead.

There is one voice in the room. I tear my eyes away from Allegra and Bruce to find the source. Andre is curled up in the opposite corner of the room, trying to wail but only succeeding in whimpering softly. He is naked and his chest has been slashed to ribbons. His leg has been removed right above the knee, and, without a tourniquet, he is bleeding freely onto the plastic-covered floor. His raw thigh stump is as bright as a cartoon steak, and I can see a circle of white bone in the middle.

Andre rolls onto his stomach to reveal hundreds of little razor blades sticking out of his back in an intricate spiral pattern. Each one is punctuated with a drop or two of blood, narrow red lines intersecting and separating again on their way to the floor. Words I heard Allegra utter that night, right before re-entering this room, echo in my head: "I could make you into a porcupine with razors for spines." His face is pale and his eyes are sunken. He's rapidly being sapped of strength. I can't help him.

As Allegra continues robotically puncturing Bruce's dead stomach, something in the corner beyond them catches my eye. A pile of parts. Pieces. A mound of gore that was once a human body. Two severed hands. Two severed feet. Two legs and two arms, each sliced away where they used to bend. The meat of the torso has been portioned into chunks and several shiny pink organs are placed neatly by their side. Her breasts were removed whole. Her head is on top of the grotesque pyramid, perched like a warning. Her long, dark hair is still intact, hanging into the viscera, soaking it all in. Her eyes are closed, and the eye shadow on them is beautiful. The woman I hit with my car. It can't be. It's impossible.

Even though her lungs are clearly identifiable on the floor beside her, the head opens its mouth, takes a deep breath, and screams.

I woke up panting, sweat sticking strands of hair to my cheeks. I was on my side facing the wall, Allegra's body curled around mine. My tank top had ridden up to my collarbones and she was lightly cupping my left breast in her right hand as she breathed peacefully. Yellow street lights were barely visible beyond the bedroom curtain, and I could tell the sky was still dark. I disentangled myself from the blankets and Allegra and carefully crawled off the bed, righting my shirt as I stood.

I leaned against the bathroom sink without turning on the overhead light. The quiet, cool room spun a few lazy rotations around me, and I closed my eyes to make it stop, but not being able to see where my body was in space made the dizziness and nausea worse. I pitched forward and threw up stomach bile and the remnants of two pastries into the sink. My stomach kept contracting, forcing me to gag and retch long after it was empty. Cold sweat dripped down my cheeks and chest even though my face was flushed red hot. My head pulsed painfully and I couldn't stop panting as if I'd just finished a 10k run. I sat on the closed toilet to avoid passing out.

I finally caught my breath and tested my ability to stand, which I did successfully without tipping too far to one side or the other. I quietly gathered my earbuds, cell phone, knitting needles, and a skein of blue yarn from the bedroom and settled onto the living room couch to wait for sunrise.

My dad and I had made plans to meet up for lunch today since I was off from work and he was supervising a construction site a few blocks away from the apartment. He texted me around eight a.m. to confirm our date, and like an idiot, I sent back a simple "Sounds great!" instead of the confession that I'd likely be crashing from lack of sleep by noon.

By the time I stepped outside, the morning chill had blown away and the sun was bright and warm. When I arrived at the small cafe, I surprised myself by noticing a small burst of energy when the aromas of freshly ground coffee and sizzling meat hit my nose. The interior of the cafe was about as far from Starbucks as it was possible to get. The counter and tables were made of sturdy wood, soft lighting and music emanated from the ceiling, and the chairs even had a little cushion to them. My body no longer ached from throwing up and my thoughts were clear.

Dad sat at the farthest table from the entrance, near a window where rays of afternoon sunlight shone onto his bushy black beard, highlighting the grays. He sipped iced tea from a tall glass, eyes unfocused and staring at nothing. He didn't notice I'd arrived until I sat down across from him.

"Hey!" he said excitedly, snapping out of his reverie. "I'm happy to see you! Feels like it's been months."

"It *has* been months," I said, smiling at Dad's signature absentmind-edness and fidgeting with the paper menus on the table. "I've missed you. Just been so busy with work, and…" I let myself trail off, not wanting him to know the reasons for my distraction. Thankfully, a waitress approached our table and eliminated the need for me to continue.

"Hey there," she says to me, smiling a pearly customer-service grin and setting a steaming mug of black coffee in front of me. She had frizzy blonde curls pulled into a ponytail, and a little of her bright red lipstick had stuck to her front tooth. "Would you like cream and sugar with this?"

"I ordered drinks before you got here," Dad explained.

"Sure, thanks," I told the waitress. "Just cream, no sugar. Thanks."

"I can't believe you're not tired of coffee after slingin' it forty hours a week," Dad said as I held the mug under my nose and inhaled.

I shrugged. "What can I say? It's my life force."

The waitress came back with my cream and took our order: two BLTs, no tomato for me, no mayo for Dad, and a basket of fries to share. After she took our menus and left, we sat in silence for several minutes.

"You look tired," Dad finally said.

"Thank you," I shot back with more sarcasm than intended.

"I don't mean it in a bad way, you just look stressed. Are you getting enough sleep?"

"I think you already know the answer to that is 'no.'"

He lowered his gaze to the tabletop. "Yeah, I know that. Guess I was hoping it would have figured itself out by now."

I wanted to laugh out loud. I loved my dad, but what a stupid thing to say. Especially considering his own, he should have known that people don't just grow out of anxiety and sleep issues. I settled for a scoff. He didn't look so great himself; he had dark circles under his eyes, and his face looked bloated and acne-ridden. His complexion was darker than usual from too many hours spent outside and his face was starting to take on a leathery appearance.

I sipped my drink and tried to think of something to say. All that came to mind was a story about how someone had rear-ended someone else in the drive-thru at work earlier that week, and then tried to pay for their coffee instead of exchanging insurance information.

"You know what? I think I *am* tired of coffee," I said, furrowing my brow and staring into the mug in front of me.

"We can get you something else to drink when the waitress comes back," Dad offered.

"No, I mean…" I sighed and brought my eyes up to meet his. "You said earlier you can't believe I'm not tired of coffee yet. But I think I am.

I can't even think of any life updates to tell you that don't involve angry customers or espresso."

Before he could answer, the waitress reappeared and set a sandwich on a white plate down in front of each of us, and a basket of steaming fries in the center of the table. I grabbed a fry and popped it in my mouth, relishing the salty crunch. I couldn't remember the last time I'd had french fries.

Dad picked up one triangular half of his sandwich and bit into the corner. When he was done chewing, he smiled at me. "Do you remember the first time you had a BLT?"

"Of course," I say. "It was at IHOP, I was probably eight? And you always got them so I just had to try one."

"When they brought it out you took the biggest bite I'd ever seen a little girl take, and you chewed it for so long I thought it had to have turned to complete mush. Then you said, very thoughtfully, 'What was the slimy thing that ruined my sandwich?'" His smile deepened to a grin, the creases in his forehead and cheeks becoming more pronounced. "You were always so outspoken. Always knew exactly what you wanted."

I scratched at my mug, unsure of what to say. How could I begin to tell Dad how far removed I was from that opinionated little girl? I still hated tomatoes, but if Allegra told me to eat one, I would probably do it without asking a single question.

Dad kept reminiscing about my childhood. "Whenever someone asked what you wanted to do when you grew up, you had a different answer. Veterinarian, architect, lawyer, bakery owner, pirate! Strangers always got a kick out of you, especially little old ladies."

We ate in companionable silence, rediscovering the familiar rhythm of hundreds of meals that had been so natural before I'd moved out. When I finished my coffee, I asked the waitress for a Sprite, and she brought me an icy can. Dad added extra salt and pepper to the fries.

As I ate my perfectly tomato-less BLT, I considered my future with Starbucks. I could continue working there full time until I got promoted to manager, which most likely came with a raise and better benefits. The company treated their employees well, and I could do a lot worse than working there until retirement, but didn't I want more?

More than, as my dad said, slinging coffee five days a week until I dropped dead? More than pretending that slinging coffee was my whole personality so I could go home afterward and help my girlfriend murder people with impunity?

"Can I get you folks anything else?" the waitress asked, appearing from nowhere.

"No, thanks," I said.

"Okay then, here's your check." She placed it on the table between Dad and me. "Whenever you're ready, you can bring this up front to pay." She retreated again.

"Hey, Dad?" I asked.

"Hey, what?" he asked back, mimicking my tone perfectly as he stood up from his seat.

"What if… When my lease is up this summer, what if I moved back home?"

Dad looked at me skeptically. "Are things not working out with Allegra?"

Well, I did let her back into my bed last night after two months of fighting, but there's still the small issue of her wanting to become the next Jeffrey Dahmer when I literally just want to live my life, I wanted to say. Instead, I went for a version of the truth that would require much less explanation.

"I was just thinking, maybe I want to go back to school and stop working so many hours. Living at home would help if I have to pay tuition, even if I start out with community college."

Dad's face broke into another grin, even bigger than before, but it quickly dimmed as if he were afraid of scaring away my ambition with too much enthusiasm.

"Bug," he says carefully, "I'd support you whether you wanted to become Supreme Court Justice or go for the Guinness World Record of longest-running Starbucks employee. But of course, you're always welcome at home. It'd actually be great to have you back."

I stood up and gave him a big hug that he wasn't expecting. It almost knocked him over, but he steadied himself on the table. The yellow safety vest he hadn't taken off before leaving work left a smear of dirt on my cheek, which I didn't notice until Dad was gone and I was outside the cafe taking a selfie with my phone. I wiped off the dirt and smiled for the camera, then posted the picture to Facebook with the caption, "Feeling optimistic!" By the time I got home, the post already had fifteen likes.

CHAPTER 17

Allegra

June 2008

As I climbed the steps leading to my high school theater, a large colorful banner caught my eye. Length spanning the entire front of the building, it read, *Welcome to the 11th Annual POWERHOUSE DANCE Recital!* The neon colors and several different fonts made my head hurt, so I turned my attention away from the banner and adjusted my dress.

At our last studio rehearsal, Andrea had hinted that guest choreographers should dress nicely for the performance since their work was being showcased. At the time, I hadn't really known what to wear, but when I got home and checked my closet, I realized there could only be one answer: the red and black dress I had worn the night we took care of Bruce. Getting the blood out of it had been surprisingly easy; I'd soaked it in cold water as soon as I'd taken it off that night, then run it through the wash with a little baking soda the next day. There were still a few additions to the original pattern, but they blended into the fabric and couldn't be identified for what they were. Evidence or not, the dress was still my most powerful outfit. Plus, the colors coordinated with Bruce's bracelet perfectly. I had added a pair of simple three-inch black heels, since I figured going barefoot would be frowned upon, and a small black purse. I'd managed to get my hair into graceful beach waves and looked, if I did say so myself, marvelous.

I felt someone staring at me. When I finished smoothing the last wrinkle from my skirt, I glanced around until I found him: someone's brother was watching me. He was probably no older than sixteen, standing with his parents and preteen sister who already had her full face of makeup on. His knees were knobby in his cargo shorts, and I could see little collections of acne from where I stood at least twenty feet away. When he realized I was looking back, he smiled, and it was so pure that I couldn't help but smirk back. His mother tried to hand him the bouquet of flowers she was holding. He reached for it without breaking eye contact with me. When I winked discreetly at him, his fingers closed around empty air and the flowers fell to the ground. When he bent to pick them up, I turned and walked inside as I considered how easy it might be to make him my next victim.

Between previous recitals and school assemblies, I'd been in this theater dozens of times. It was the nicest theater in our little area of Mesa that sat more than one hundred people. Rows of unoccupied blue velvet seats and wooden armrests greeted me as I made my way through the house and into the backstage area. Only about half of the overhead lights had been turned on, and aside from one lighting tech shuffling papers in his booth, the area was empty.

The dressing rooms were another story completely. As soon as I climbed the steps to the stage and passed through the thick black door separating the audience from the performers, my senses were lovingly assaulted with familiar chaos. Every single fluorescent light on the ceiling glowed, along with the even brighter shine of vanity lighting on the mirrors. Girls in various stages of dress were talking, laughing, singing, yelling, gossiping, playing card games, examining their makeup in the mirrors, making sure they still didn't have a run in their tights, and going over their dances one last time. I accidentally walked into a thick cloud of hairspray and coughed loudly. Someone yelled "Oh, sorry!" before their voice was drowned out by someone else's hair dryer.

After the initial confusion of walking into the room, I was able to differentiate the people well enough to find my group. The six members of our dance team had commandeered a corner with two mirrored vanity stations and a shallow counter. Everyone's black dance bags had been piled underneath the counter and chairs to make more room for the people.

"Allegra!" Ashley waved as I found a chair and sat down. Her hair and makeup were already flawlessly finished, her freckles covered by a thick layer of foundation. The group's first dance would be mine, so they were already dressed in their costumes: black leggings, purple tank tops, see-through black lace overshirts, and black jazz shoes.

After the initial greetings, the girls started chattering amongst themselves, and I allowed myself to zone out and enjoy the hustle and bustle of the dressing room. The scents of makeup, body spray, hair products, and the nervous sweat of first-time performers intermingled to form an aroma not found anywhere else. Just as the atmosphere began to transform into comforting white noise, I felt a warm hand on my shoulder and snapped back to reality. I turned around and gasped in surprise.

"Allegra?" Nova said, her hand remaining on my shoulder after I turned around. "I thought that was you. Remember me?"

"I— Of course. Nova. What are you…"

"Doing here? I teach at Powerhouse!"

"But you live in California…"

"I go to ASU now," she explained. "I've been in Tempe since last August."

"You look amazing," I say, and it's true. Her short, dark hair had been buzzed on both sides, forming a style between faux-hawk and mohawk. She was also dressed in street clothes, but hers were more casual than mine: black jeans, a nice button-down blouse with yellow flowers, and shiny magenta Doc Martens. Her body, still beautifully toned, was more curvaceous than I remembered.

"Holy shit. I never thought I'd see you again. Damn. How are you? What are *you* doing here? I haven't seen you around the studio, do you teach there?"

"No, this is my school. They let the dance team perform in exchange for using our theater." My heart was beating hard and my hands were shaking. I plunged them under my thighs so she wouldn't see.

"Oh yeah, I think someone told me that's how we scored this sweet spot."

I noticed that she still hadn't removed her hand from my shoulder. If she had been anyone else I would have hated this kind of extended contact, but I didn't want it to end.

"Um, Miss Nova?" A little girl in a pink leotard and tights, maybe about seven years old, came up behind Nova and tapped her on the hip. "I can't find the little flower for my hair, and my mom said maybe she left it at home and wants to know if you have any extras."

Nova's demeanor immediately shifted from social to professional.

"Of course, Taylor. They're in my car, give me a minute and I'll go grab them."

The child smiled widely, showing us several missing teeth, and then ran away without another word.

"Well," Nova said to me with a shrug, "duty calls. But, can we meet up later?"

"Of course," I said, and she was gone.

Nova walked away, and I leaned forward to pull my still-shaking hands out from under my legs. I told my group I would go grab us a stack of programs and left the dressing room.

I wandered around backstage for at least twenty minutes, lost in thoughts of Nova. What, if anything, did seeing her again mean for my life? Our connection was obvious and palpable, unlike anything I'd ever experienced. I couldn't believe her mere presence had caught me so off guard. This was only the second time we'd ever seen each other, but she felt like a long-lost love.

Holy shit. Love? Am I even capable of love? The word came out of nowhere but rang incredibly true. Even though I often told Robin I loved her, I'd never stopped to analyze whether I really loved anyone. It was just something I knew she wanted to hear. Now, I had apparently fallen in actual love with a veritable stranger. Great.

I tried to distract myself by checking my phone. I had a text from Toby: *Visited mom at the hospital today. Man that place is depressing.* I didn't know what to say, so I closed the message and dropped my phone back into my purse.

Our mom had been admitted to inpatient psychiatric care in May following a suicide attempt. I didn't have too many details since my dad was too busy with visits, working his overnights, and taking care of Toby to keep me updated, but Toby sent me little messages like this every once in a while. From what I had gathered, Mom started feeling bad right after Easter and couldn't figure out why. Within a couple weeks, she was no longer able to make it through a day without a panic attack, dissociative episode, or depression so severe that she slept for days.

According to Toby, she had mentioned several times that she couldn't figure out what was happening since she'd been on the same medication without any incidents for years. Her work had finally suggested she take a leave of absence to get back on track, and she was so distraught that instead of calling her doctor, she crashed her car into a freeway median on the way home. Her only injuries were a broken leg and a mild concussion, but when the hospital staff figured out she had done it on purpose as a suicide attempt, they sent her to the psych floor immediately, and she'd been there ever since.

I knew I should be a more supportive big sister. I should have answered Toby and asked if he wanted to finally go on the birthday shopping trip I'd promised and never delivered, or at least told him everything was going to be okay with Mom. I hadn't expected that replacing her pills with placebos would result in a suicide attempt—at least, not so quickly—but there were two pieces of good news attached to this purported tragedy. First, she *didn't* die, and her injuries were minor, and she was most likely actually getting the meds she needed in the hospital, so she would be back to normal again in no time. Second, all this was so distracting that she had probably forgotten all about me and Bruce's bracelet. It was a win-win.

When I got back to the dressing room with a stack of programs I'd swiped from an unoccupied usher's station, Andrea was in the dressing room making sure our whole group was present and accounted for. She wore black from hat to boots, her long black hair gathered into a messier-than-usual version of her signature messy bun, and clutched the largest size of iced Starbucks drink in one hand. The best thing about being visiting guests, not members of the dance studio hosting the recital, was that we could pretty much do whatever we wanted until it was time to go onstage. We were invited, but not required, to participate in the big group warmup and reading of notes from the last dress rehearsal. Of course, Andrea encouraged us to network with the dance studio kids, but it wasn't mandatory.

Checking the show order in one of the programs, I noticed Nova's class of little ones was the second number in the first act, and mine was ninth. At least we'd get it over with early, but as teachers, we would still need to stick around until the end of the show to be presented with 'surprise' flowers during the curtain call.

A crackling noise came from the ceiling, and then a muffled voice came out through the built-in speakers: "Attention performers, we are five minutes to curtain. Five minutes."

A discordant chorus of, "THANK YOU, FIVE!!!" rang through the dressing room as almost every dancer screamed it at the ceiling.

"You guys know he can't hear you, right?" An annoyed preteen asked her peers. She was quickly shot down by a chorus of voices defending the tradition of loudly and obnoxiously confirming you had heard the stage manager's time warning.

The door opened and Nova stuck her head into the room, looked around, and then closed the door without entering. She looked busy and stressed, but I followed anyway. When I got out the door, she was already several feet in front of me, power-walking, and clearly looking for someone.

"Nova!" I called.

She turned around and her face softened from its tense, stressed expression. "Hi. I can't talk right now, one of my kids is missing."

"Like, *missing*, missing?"

"Oh god no, she's probably just with her mom or something, but I have to get the group together. We're second!" The tense expression was back and more intense than before.

"Do you have an assistant teacher, or a class parent, or something?"

"Yeah, my assistant is with the rest of the class and she knows where they need to be and when. I just need to find Taylor."

"The same one who left her flower at home? Dang, she's having a bad day."

Nova laughed. "Nah, she's always like this. Her mom is totally scatterbrained. I just hope I can find her before—"

"Miss Nova!" The little voice came from behind me. I turned around to see Taylor holding the hand of a frazzled-looking woman whose other arm struggled to contain a screaming infant. "Miss Nova! We went to the smelly toilets in the basement and then my baby brother woke up while Mommy was trying to put my leotard back on me!"

"Sorry," the woman says, trying to be heard over the baby. "All the bathrooms up here were full, and she said it was an emergency."

Nova's body noticeably relaxed as she breathed a huge sigh of relief. "Okay, it's okay, I'm just glad you're back."

"Okay, sweetie," Taylor's mom said. "Have *such* a fun time on stage. I'll be out there watching with Daddy and your brothers!" Taylor's mom gave her a quick one-armed hug and then nudged her toward Nova, who took her hand and started to lead her back to the dressing room. I didn't have anything better to do, so I followed them.

In the hallway between the stage and dressing rooms, we encountered the rest of their class being led single-file by a teenager dressed as a ladybug. Twelve little girls in matching pink leotards and tights, pink tutus, and pink flowers stuck in their buns. The hairstyle varied in expertise from child to child, with some tight and gelled down to prevent any wisps of hair from escaping, while others were pretty much just ponytails bobby pinned into a vaguely round shape.

"Go ahead and get in line," Nova told Taylor, who scurried to join her class.

The ladybug led the kids backstage with Nova and me bringing up the rear of the group. The ladybug reminded them to be quiet backstage, but once they were in the wings, almost all of them started whispering and giggling excitedly.

Before long, the house lights dimmed and the stage lights came up on the first act. It was one of the studio's teen tap classes with an upbeat routine to "Big Noise from Winnetka," dressed in jeans and highlighter-colored shirts. I set my purse on a nearby table and took Nova's left hand with my right, and I swear the contact produced a few high-voltage sparks. Her eyes kept following the dancers on stage, but after a few seconds, she interlaced our fingers.

The song ended and the stage went black, cueing momentary whispered commotion as the tappers exited the stage and Nova's kids realized it was their turn next. The ladybug got the kids back into their line, ready to make their entrance.

As her kids carefully turned and leapt to "Waltz of the Flowers," Nova leaned close and whispered in my ear. "When they're done, do you wanna take a walk with me?"

"My dance is in a few more, but yeah," I whispered back.

"It doesn't have to take that long." Her smirk glowed pink in the reflection of the stage lights.

The song ended, and the little ones struck their final pose. When the lights went down, all thirteen girls sprinted off the stage and into the waiting arms of Nova and her ladybug assistant, before the assistant led the class back to the dressing room to meet their parents. Nova took my hand again and led me away from the side of the stage.

This theater had a basement with seldom-used bathrooms, dressing rooms, and practice rooms that contained pianos. She seemed to know the way to this secluded area almost as well as I did. I tried each door knob with no luck as we walked down the bleak hallway, looking for someplace we could stop and sit.

"So," Nova said with an inquisitive expression as she watched me try doors. "When I asked to friend you on Facebook, you didn't mention that you're hardly ever online."

"Oh, didn't I?" I tried another locked door, then turned to smile at her. "Must have slipped my mind."

"Seriously though," she continued. "I wish we'd been able to stay in touch. You didn't get any of the messages I sent? The messenger system told me you read them."

"Well, the messenger system is a tattletale." My tone was mock-annoyed and I smiled to make it even more obvious this was a joke. I didn't know what to say. Of course I had gotten the messages. I'd even considered responding. But she conjured so many confusing feelings in me when we met, and I hadn't been ready to confront them. Maybe I still wasn't.

Finally, after trying at least seven doors, one of the creaky metal knobs gave way and let me into a dusty ten-foot-square practice room with a tile floor and a wooden piano. Nova sat at the piano and started plinking tunelessly. I leaned my back against the wall and slid down until I was sitting on the floor with my knees against my chest.

"I didn't know you played piano," I said.

"You don't know most things about me," she replied. "There are pictures of me playing on Facebook."

She smirked and caught my gaze out of the corner of her eye and held it for several seconds to make sure I'd understood the pointed jab before refocusing on the black and white keys. She tried a slow, plodding version of "Für Elise", because that or "Chopsticks", or both, were apparently the law whenever you sat behind a piano and had ever taken a lesson in your life. I hummed along to the discord. This piano was seriously out of tune. I wondered how long since anyone had used it.

"*Anyway*," I said, emphasizing my need to move on with the conversation. "What have you been up to for the last year?"

"Oh… Ya know…" She sighed and looked at the ceiling like she was about to tell a long, complicated story. "Finished high school. Went to ASU. Got this job at Powerhouse and used most of my paychecks on tattoos. Started dating someone and had my heart brutally stepped on and ground into a million tiny dust particles… And then it's now." She smirked. "And you?"

"'Me' what?" I asked, playing dumb.

"What have you been doing? Are you seeing anyone?"

"No. Well, yeah, kind of. Yeah."

"Sounds complicated," Nova said, searching my face for answers.

"I'm living with someone. We've been together for a while, but… It's not going great these days."

"Is he an asshole or something?"

"Why do you assume it's a 'he'?"

"Isn't it?"

Now it was my turn to smirk with hidden information. "Her name is Robin."

If Nova had been a cartoon character, her jaw would have fallen all the way to the floor as her eyes bugged out of her head. She had probably spent the last year thinking I was a straight girl who saw her as a fluke and would be settling down with a man any day now. After a few seconds readjusting her view of me, she recovered her composure and asked why my relationship wasn't going well.

"Honestly, I don't even know if you can call it a relationship anymore. She was upset about something I did, and then we kinda made up a couple months ago, but I can tell it probably won't last too much longer."

"Well, if you loved each other enough to move in together, maybe there's still something there and you just need to find it again." She finally stopped plunking the piano keys and moved from the piano bench to sit on the floor next to me.

"We were kinda living together *before* we got together."

She chortled. "You're screwing your roommate?"

"No! Not exactly. Well…" I smiled sheepishly at the way she twisted my words and the entertained look on her face. "We hooked up, then decided to just be friends, then moved in together as friends, *then* started dating after living together for a while."

"I see," Nova said, nodding slowly.

"She had to break up with her boyfriend first," I explained.

"I was right, that is complicated." She took my hand and interlaced our fingers the way she had backstage.

I glanced pointedly at our hands. "Yes, and *this* isn't complicating things more," I said sarcastically.

"Sorry," she said, taking her hand back. "You spent the last five minutes telling me about your relationship and then… I shouldn't have."

"I didn't say that," I said softly.

I leaned over and closed the few inches of distance between us. Nova kissed me back, uninhibited, immediately hungry. As soon as I tasted her tongue, I was transported in my mind back to the hotel where we met, the pressure of her fingers on the back of my neck as I hovered over her on the perfectly made bed, the thrill of missing a class to stay with her for just a few more minutes. *Have you ever been choked during sex?* I had asked her. The answer, then, had been no. I wondered if it was different now.

Before I knew it, we were horizontal and panting on the tile floor, my hand snaking up her shirt and searching for the clasp of her bra. I wasn't necessarily proud of the way I was losing control, but Nova had that effect on me. She made me want to break the rules.

I broke my mouth away from hers and nibbled and licked my way down her neck and chest, unbuttoning her blouse until I could see the tan bra underneath.

"Ooh, careful, sorry," she said, gingerly easing my face away from her left breast. "My new tattoo is still tender." She showed me the collection of flowers that extended from her hip to just underneath her bra. The skin under the outlines was raised, and some parts of her skin were pinker than the rest. I'd never seen a brand new tattoo before but didn't think this one could be more than a week or two old.

"I'll be careful," I said quietly. I succeeded in unhooking her bra and gently pushed it out of my way. When I did so, I noticed another, much smaller and older tattoo of a single word following the curve under her breast: *sonder*. Before I could comment on the tattoo, Nova guided my face back to hers with greedy hands.

During our next breathing break, I stroked her delicate neck and bare chest with my fingertips, delighting each time it made her shudder. I tested gently, ever so gently, applying a little pressure here and there. Her breathing became more ragged and she giggled with anticipatory excitement. I used my thumb and middle finger to squeeze her neck from both sides at once, and she grabbed my hair and pulled me in for a long kiss.

"Just make sure to press on the sides, not the front," she said, adjusting my grip. Nova giving me pointers on how to choke her was more surprising than the fact that she didn't shake off my grip immediately when I tried. Sensing my confusion, she explained, "The ex I told you about was really into BDSM. I learned some stuff."

I left my hand around her neck, varying pressure every few seconds and listening to the way her breath changed. She didn't seem afraid at all, possibly assuming that if I was doing this, I had at least as much BDSM knowledge or experience as her ex. I pressed hard on the front of her throat and she grunted in sudden pain.

"The side, the side," she tried to say. "Stop... Alleg..."

The words came out somewhere between a moan and a whisper. I didn't respond. She tried to inhale, eyes growing wide with effort. The fist that was in my hair grasped it tightly, trying to hurt me badly enough to release my grip, but it didn't work. She was already too weak from lack of oxygen, a pleasant surprise I hadn't expected to happen so quickly. I maintained my grip as I counted thirty beats of her heart, watching her eyes flutter closed in defeat, then relaxed and shook the muscle cramp out of my hand. I used two fingers to check the pulse in her neck; it was weak but wouldn't be stopping any time soon.

I briefly considered restraining her somehow, so she wouldn't try to run away immediately upon waking up and tell someone what I'd done, but decided against it. I didn't think the situation would end up that serious. While she was unconscious, I stayed straddling her hips and studied her face. Nova wasn't traditionally beautiful, but I'd challenge anyone with even a slight attraction to women to look away from her interestingly constructed face. She had a long, angular nose that didn't quite match up with her small bow lips. Her open eyes were a piercing aquamarine, but while they were closed I got to admire the perfect job she had done on her eye shadow. It was gray and smoky near her lashes to blend with her eyeliner, then transitioned into a subtle yellow to match the flowers in her blouse. The blouse that was now abandoned next to her on the floor, collecting dust that would probably have to be dry-cleaned out of the fabric.

I only noticed that my fingers were still on her neck, monitoring her pulse as her heart rapidly tried to regulate itself, when she gasped violently and tried to sit up. When she realized I was still sitting on top of her, she collapsed back onto the ground. Now that she was awake, her breathing was more irregular than before, but it had lost all the zeal. I matched a few of my breaths to hers, and then adopted my own panicked rhythm, as if I'd been freaking out since she first lost consciousness. She tried to talk, probably to tell me to get off her, but it came out in a raspy, unintelligible whisper. I grabbed her blouse and hid it behind my back as she got her bearings.

"What the *fuck*," she asked in her new raspy voice that hardly sounded human at all. "I said the *sides*."

"I'm sorry!" I said, too loudly. "I'm so sorry, I…" I took a deep breath and tried to look like I was doing my best to calm down now that she was back. "I guess I'm not as good at that as I thought."

Nova considered my words and stared at me for a few seconds as she rubbed her neck. "It happens, I guess. But damn. I thought you knew what you were doing… You seem to have your wits about you in every other situation so I just assumed."

"Nova…" I put my open palm on her shoulder. She didn't flinch away. That was a good sign. "I lost control. I didn't mean to. Guess you just have that effect on me." I tried to smile, but the true words tasted bad as they left my mouth and I could only manage a grimace.

I rolled off her lap, still holding her shirt behind my back, and stood up. She followed my lead and put her bra back on properly with her back to me.

"We should probably get back upstairs. Isn't your dance soon?"

"Yeah," I said with a shrug, "but they're not babies. I'm sure they can get to the wings on their own, plus their real teacher is there if anything goes wrong."

Nova readily accepted my answer and moved to open the door and leave. She didn't even seem to register that she wasn't wearing a shirt. I didn't want her to go yet. "How will you explain your voice?" I asked, sure this would keep her here longer.

She shrugged, nonplussed. "I can just say I was yelling and screaming for all the dances in the first act. Wouldn't be the first time."

I took her hand and pulled gently so she had to either resist or walk the three steps across the room. Within seconds she was in front of me again and I passionately kissed her. Her arms encircled my waist, and I draped mine casually around her neck. Her shirt hung casually down her back, dangling from one of my hands. Without breaking the kiss, she maneuvered our position until I was backed against the wall. I allowed it for a few seconds before rotating us just enough that I could use my body weight to press her into the wall. She turned her back to me. I lowered one of her bra straps and kissed her bare shoulder.

"I have a question," she rasped.

"Yeah?"

"What did you do to your girlfriend?"

"What do you mean?" I asked, distracted. I had no idea what she was talking about or why she was bringing it up now.

"You said you did something that made your girlfriend upset and now it might be over. What did you do?"

I held the blouse up to Nova's back like I was going to help her put it on. In one fluid movement that I would have to remind myself to be proud of later, I scrunched the shirt into a makeshift rope, looped it around her neck from behind, and twisted the two ends together right above the beginning of her spine.

"That's not funny," she strained to say, trying to squirm out of my grasp. "Not when I just passed out from imperfect asphyxiation."

"It's not supposed to be funny," I said quietly. I held the shirt in place in a way that allowed her to breathe a little, as long as she stayed completely still. I twisted the two ends around each other a few times, and she audibly gagged.

"To answer your question," I whispered in her ear, "I killed someone. I think my girlfriend is just having second thoughts about helping me do it."

As her air supply was cut off, Nova clawed at the wall with her bitten, unpolished fingernails until a few chunks of white paint bounced off her boots and collected at her feet. She clenched her jaw in concentration. When she tried to reach behind herself and claw at me, I had no choice but to grab her fauxhawk and bash her forehead into the wall as hard as I could. This resulted in a freely bleeding gash right above her eyebrow and a much more pliable victim. I twisted the fabric until I couldn't anymore, pushing past the ache setting into my fingers and thighs as the minutes of bracing myself against her dragged on. At one point, I heard a crack and thought I may have broken her neck, but when I momentarily released pressure on the shirt, it was still sturdy enough to hold her head up. I tightened my grip again and her face turned from the shocking white pallor of the terrified to the slight blue tinge of someone who had lost the battle for their life. Her jaw relaxed and her mouth fell weakly open. I was momentarily disappointed that I wouldn't get to look into her eyes as she took her last breath, but with my entire body pressed against hers, I had something better: a visceral front row seat.

She wasn't fighting me anymore. Not at all. Obviously, her fate was sealed and trying to get away was pointless. I hadn't expected Nova to be one to just roll over and accept her death, but at least in her last few moments, she was recognizing that I was the one in control—and had been the entire time. I had been in control of her since we met; the 'sonder' tattoo was proof she had never stopped thinking of me since that afternoon in her hotel room. I worked two fingers under the tightly wound fabric and found the pulse in her neck. It wasn't rapid anymore. There was no rhythm to her pulse at all. There was more space between beats each time until finally, the next beat never came.

I wasn't totally sure that Nova was dead until her knees gave way and I had to guide her body back onto the floor. Even though I hadn't just let the body drop, it fell at a weird angle that wouldn't have been comfortable if she had still been alive. As soon as I saw the darker spot at the crotch of her black jeans, I realized I could smell the urine. What a pathetic way to be discovered. Alone on the dirty floor of some tiny room in the basement of a high school theater in just your bra and wet pants, shirt fatally tied around your neck by someone you thought you could trust even though you had no real reason to. I took out my phone and snapped a picture. Looking at it on the phone screen, it looked like a Jack the Ripper crime scene photo. Even more so after applying the sepia filter and cropping the piano leg out of the background.

I noticed for the first time that she was wearing a couple of bracelets on each wrist. I hastily took the one that looked easiest to remove, sturdy wooden beads held together with a durable elastic cord, then locked the door from the inside and exited the room. I wondered how long it would be until she was discovered. I slid her bracelet onto my wrist next to Bruce's. The chances of someone noticing my jewelry and connecting it with what they had seen Nova wearing earlier was there, but it was very slim, and I was high enough on adrenaline and confidence not to care.

Why did I do that? I asked myself as I made my way up the stairs and back to the backstage area. Maybe I had been freaked out about the level of inexplicable intimacy Nova and I had from the beginning. Maybe I had subconsciously wanted to kill her so no one could tell Robin I cheated on her. *Maybe,* I reasoned, *this is just who I am.*

I didn't want to stay to watch my group. I didn't want to participate in this stupid recital anymore. My class was old enough not to need their hands held between the dressing room and the stage, and I didn't want to be around if someone else ventured to the basement and found Nova's body. I figured there was a fifty/fifty chance leaving the building without telling anyone I was going would make me look guiltier than sticking around and acting natural, but in the unlikely event that she was discovered before the end of the show, I also didn't trust myself to lie convincingly about the last time I had seen her. Not when it came to Nova.

My purse was undisturbed on the table at the side of the stage. I grabbed it and hustled out of the building, avoiding eye contact with the few people hanging out in the lobby instead of watching the show.

On the bus home, I texted Andrea: *Sorry I had to leave unexpectedly. My mom is in the hospital. Let me know how my number went?* It wasn't technically a lie, and it would pull on Andrea's heartstrings hard enough for her not to be angry at me for leaving. Predictably, Andrea texted back within minutes with well wishes for my mom and assurance that my leaving was no problem. She used so many exclamation points that I could hear her cloyingly upbeat tone as I read the messages.

The bus stopped to let a few people off, then lurched forward again. I tried to convince myself this would be fine. That I couldn't be connected to Nova's murder any more than anyone else in the building that day. That Mom wouldn't figure out I was the reason for her sudden relapse. That Robin and I would eventually get back to normal. I tried, but in the back of my mind, I knew these things wouldn't be true for long if I stayed in Arizona. I much more easily connected with Nova's murder than Bruce's. I was sure I could get Robin to lie for me if I needed an alibi, but this was not necessarily a desirable situation for me to be in. I had never wanted to get this close to my victims. *The only way serial killers achieve the "serial" part is by being a lot smarter than I just was*, I criticized in my head. The only option was for Robin and me to leave, get new identities, and start over somewhere new.

I also knew that wherever we ended up, I would have to keep killing. It was nonnegotiable. Being with Nova in that practice room had exhilarated me more than anything had since Bruce. Feeling the pulsating veins in her neck and pressing myself against her as she lost consciousness for the final time had finally given me dominance over my feelings for her. I had absorbed her lust, her terror, and her misguided confidence. When I locked her in that room and left her there alone, I left the potential for our love with her and carried her power away with me. And now it was time to go.

CHAPTER 18

Robin

June 2008

Allegra stalked into the apartment, glamorous as always when she wore that red and black dress, as I heated up a frozen dinner in the kitchen. Without greeting me or even acknowledging I was home, she gathered the shirts and sweaters slung over the back of the living room couch and threw them into a basket full of other clothes. I followed her with silent curiosity as she took it into her bedroom and emptied every drawer of her dresser into the basket, now overflowing. She stood up and disappeared into her closet, where I heard her rummaging and mumbling. Her tone inside the closet was a little unhinged, but when she emerged with an armful of dresses on hangers she looked exactly as calm as she usually did. She dropped the dresses on the bed and went back to the closet for a large suitcase I hadn't seen since we moved in.

"What are you doing?" I asked. She looked up at me, and I think that was truly the first moment she realized I had been watching her since she came in. My heart started beating so hard that I could feel it knocking against my bones. There was something wrong with her, but I couldn't pinpoint what it was.

"Get packed, it's time to move," she said matter-of-factly.

"Um…" Her declaration caught me by such surprise that I couldn't think of a response.

"Come on, get moving. We can leave tonight. Or bright and early tomorrow morning." She started stuffing the dresses into the suitcase.

I took her by the shoulders, forcing her to stop the constant movement. "Allegra, what are you talking about? The lease isn't up for another two months. Did something happen tonight? Are you losing it? What's going on?"

Even though my grip on her shoulders prevented her from moving around the room, Allegra's fingers and wrists still twitched impatiently and her gaze was focused on the suitcase. After a few seconds, she made eye contact with me again and her face transformed into a soft, neutral expression. At that moment, she was almost the Ally I fell in love with. But then she smiled and slowly stretched the grin too far. Her face distorted until it was closer to the one she had made in my dream as she pierced oozing black holes in Bruce's stomach. The dull popping sound of skin giving way to a weapon echoed in my ears as images from the dream flashed through my head in rapid succession.

"Don't you hate it here? We've talked about moving out of Arizona so many times. Let's do it right now, just get away in the dead of night like Thelma and Louise!"

"If you're planning for our ending to be like theirs, we probably don't need to bother packing much," I said sarcastically.

"Fine, Bonnie and Clyde."

"My previous statement still stands. Anyway, we can't just leave. The apartment office has our social security numbers, they can track us down and charge us for abandoning our contract."

"Not if we just disappear."

I used the grip I still had on her shoulders to steer her toward the mattress and make her sit down. "Tell me what's happening."

Allegra stared at her lap for a long time, either trying to get her thoughts straight or working out a lie to tell me. She took a few deep breaths as if she was about to say something, but let them out defeatedly each time.

"I killed someone," she finally said, a colossal letdown after all that buildup.

"Yeah, I know," I said, nodding. "I was there, remember?"

"No—" she started to say.

"It was months ago," I continued as if she hadn't said anything. "Why the sudden need to get away?"

"I killed someone…else. Tonight."

My vision immediately went fuzzy. My ears started ringing and every inch of skin on my body started to tingle. Even without any more information, anxiety immediately froze me to the spot. If she hadn't wanted to flee after pouring someone's liquified remains down our toilet, how much worse could this murder be?

"No, you didn't. You're messing with me. Right?"

"I promise, I'm not messing with you."

"But… How could you have? It's a theater, Ally. With a recital going on inside of it. Hundreds of witnesses! What did you do, pull an *Interview With a Vampire* and pretend it was all just part of the show?"

She smiled, clearly entertained by the reference. "Of course not. There were no witnesses, and my fingerprints are nowhere in the system. Don't freak out," she said, even though I was clearly freaking out already. "I think it's gonna be okay if we just get out of here. We can start over fresh, somewhere that no one pays attention… Like Nebraska. Or West Virginia."

"I think people pay attention in West Virginia."

"Okay then, Nebraska it is. There's nothing there but corn."

"I don't want to go anywhere," I said. "At least, not right now. Definitely not *tonight*. There's no plan, no destination… Anyway, wouldn't the cops be after you if you'd killed someone in public? I know you said no witnesses, but there's never *no* witnesses. You should know that. You watch more true crime than anyone I've ever seen."

She pulled her cell phone out of her dress pocket and started pressing buttons.

"You didn't…" I shook my head in disbelief.

"Hang on a second, I'll show you."

I kept shaking my head. "No. Allegra, you didn't. You…took a picture of it?"

She nodded, getting excited to show me. Finally, she turned the screen and I saw the image before I could tell myself not to look. A girl about our age, topless with a shirt knotted around her neck, eyes closed, clearly dead. She bore a gruesome similarity to the girl I'd hit with my car, or maybe it was just the makeup.

"I— Is this edited?"

"Yeah. I think it looks cooler that way."

I realized I was still shaking my head but didn't make any effort to stop. "Jesus fucking Christ," I whispered. "I just… Fuck. What the… What the fuck."

"Believe me now?" she asked smugly as she put her phone away.

I didn't need to say anything. She knew the answer.

"What if someone looks in your phone?"

"They won't. I'm going to wipe it clean and then throw it away. I just wanted to look at this a little longer before I do."

"Who even is that girl?" I asked, close to tears.

"Just someone from the dance studio that uses our space. It doesn't matter. Are you coming with or what?" She stood up like she was ready to walk out the door right that minute. I stayed rooted to my spot on the bed.

"No."

"That's okay, it'll probably look suspicious if we both disappear at the same time." She started moving again, transferring the contents of the overflowing basket into the suitcase. "You should stay and tie up loose ends with work and your dad. Come join me in a week or so. I'll figure out a way to tell you where I end up."

I fixed my eyes on the knees of my jeans, focusing on the denim so I could say what I needed to say. "No. I mean no, I'm not coming. At all."

Allegra scoffed. "Oh yeah? And what are you gonna do instead?" She finished with the clothes and crossed her arms across her chest, impatiently waiting for my answer.

I shrugged, all my confidence immediately gone after dropping the bomb. "Move back in with my dad. Go to school. I dunno… Be normal. I'm not cut out for a life of crime."

Allegra crossed the room and kneeled on the floor in front of me. She looked up at me and locked her enormous eyes with mine, simultaneously providing me with a generous glimpse of cleavage, which produced the perplexingly perfect combination of innocent and enticing. She gently rested her hands on my knees.

"Aw. Robin," she said sympathetically, without breaking eye contact. "You're not cut out for much of a life at all. Not without me."

I searched her eyes, trying to figure out if this cruelty had been inside her since the beginning. I didn't want to believe that Allegra—Ally—the first person I'd loved, the person who knew all my secrets including those that could ruin me—the one I had shared a life and a bed with for almost a year, was that vicious. Even though I had literally seen her kick a dead body, enraged that he had the audacity to bleed out before she was finished playing with him, I still couldn't believe this was what she really thought of me. I briefly considered that she might break into a grin and tell me this had all been a joke. She hadn't killed anyone tonight, and she wasn't planning to do it ever again. "Wasn't that convincing?" she would ask with a laugh, and then we could go watch TV, and have sex, and eat croissants in our underwear, and everything would be normal again. But I knew that wasn't going to happen—now or ever.

I didn't have anything to say to that, so I just got up and left the room. I had succeeded in telling Ally that I wasn't coming with her. Now, all I had to do was the hardest part: really not go. I wandered into the kitchen and started a pot of the new espresso blend that had just come in at work. If it was going to be a long, sleepless night, at least it would smell like coffee in here. The tears that had threatened when she'd shown me the picture overflowed as I scooped grounds into the filter, filled the glass pot from the sink, and poured it into the reservoir. I leaned over the sink and pretended to sort the dirty dishes into piles for the dishwasher, trying to ignore my tight throat and bleary eyes.

It took Allegra about an hour to gather everything she wanted to bring and stuff it into her one suitcase, the only piece of luggage that would be manageable for running away without a car. She also made several trips to the dumpster to dispose of whatever she wouldn't be bringing, correctly assuming I wouldn't want to clean up after her when I moved out. When she walked out the door for the last time, I heard the door slam but didn't see her leave. I decided that was for the best.

While wandering around the apartment, *my* apartment for the next two months, I noticed that Allegra had left something on her bed. I approached her otherwise-empty mattress and saw it was the gray scarf I had made her, still crusty on one corner where it had soaked up a fair amount of Bruce's blood. It was folded neatly and two other items lay on top: one was the pill bottle containing what was left of her mom's pills, and the other was a note written on a sticky note from the pad we kept in the kitchen.

Robin, You get one more chance. I'll call tonight and let you know where I'm headed. See you soon. XO, A.

"Ha, fuck that," I said aloud, crumpling the note into the tiniest ball I could and stuffing it into the pocket of my jeans. I grabbed the scarf and the bottle and left the room. I tossed three of the pills into my mouth and chewed until they were dry, bitter dust. In the bathroom, I left the pills and took a travel-size bottle of hand sanitizer and the long-handled lighter we used to light candles.

I walked down the outdoor stairs into the courtyard of the apartment complex. It was a very small, not very well-kept area with a few patches of grass, a walking path, and a dispenser for plastic bags to pick up your dog's poop. It also had a couple of grills for resident use, one of which I approached to find the charred remains of a chicken wing on a very dirty grate. Clearly whoever had used it last had not heeded the *Keep Our Amenities Nice—Please Clean Up When You Leave* sign.

The other grill was relatively clean, and I didn't need it to be pristine. I tossed the scarf onto the grate and poured the whole little container of sanitizer onto it, making sure to massage it into the unabsorbent acrylic yarn. I had made this stupid scarf for Allegra as a way to show how much I loved her when I couldn't verbalize it. It was something comforting that had taken hours of work, attention, and love, and it represented all the work I wanted to put into our relationship. I'd thought she liked it—thought she liked me—but now here I was, alone at night with my knitting once again.

I took a couple of steps back, making sure I was only as close as I needed to be for the flame of the lighter to touch the edge of the scarf. Between the alcohol in the sanitizer and the cheap acrylic yarn, the scarf caught fire immediately and burned with satisfying greenish-yellow flames. It produced a strong, foul chemical smell and a few tendrils of thick black smoke floated away from the grill and into the black night sky.

The fire put itself out when it had nothing left to destroy, which was good because I hadn't had the foresight to bring water in case the flames got out of control. Like everything else that had happened since I met Allegra, I wasn't thinking about safety or consequences until it was potentially too late. I stared at the grill until the fire was completely gone. Then I brushed the piles of ash and pieces of melted yarn off the grate with my bare hands, leaving them streaked black. I rubbed my palms on my pants and headed back up the stairs to my apartment. Getting rid of the last piece of evidence from Bruce—and from my and Allegra's relationship— had taken no time at all. My buzz from the pills hadn't even kicked in yet when I settled into my room to watch TV, sip hot coffee, and knit the night away.

CHAPTER 19

Allegra

June 2008

Once it became clear that Robin wouldn't be coming with me right now, but that she also wouldn't try to stop me from leaving, I decided to take my time packing. I spent a long time in the bathroom reapplying my makeup and recreating the beach waves from earlier that day. I left on the dress and heels because beauty was more important than comfort tonight. The scent of strong coffee wafted under the bathroom door, ruining the usually calming effect my favorite cherry blossom body spray had on me.

No one should ever underestimate the skill and balance it takes to get an enormous suitcase down two flights of outdoor stairs while wearing three-inch heels. By the time I was out of the apartment complex and down the street, I was already limping and I knew my mascara was smudged even though I couldn't see it. Good thing it was dark outside. I was a little pissed that I had to walk twenty stupid minutes to the Greyhound bus station, a process that would undoubtedly make me look worse with every step.

The goal my eveningwear was supposed to achieve was a kind of dazzle camouflage. Everyone would remember the overdressed, imposing blonde woman who didn't quite belong on their bus, but no one would connect her with the almost-nineteen-year-old they saw on the evening news who was wanted for questioning in connection with a murder at a dance recital (there hadn't been any news yet but it was only a matter of time). That girl was probably hiding out somewhere in the least conspicuous jeans and hoodie she could find.

At the Greyhound station, I bought a ticket to Portland, Oregon, with cash. I didn't have a specific reason why I'd chosen Oregon. It seemed to be the most opposite climate to Arizona, and over twenty-four hours on a bus would provide plenty of time for me to figure out my next move.

I ducked into the bathroom and checked my appearance in the mirror, finding that I had been right about the mascara. I did my best to fix it with the few pieces of makeup I kept in my purse, not wanting to wrestle my larger case out of the suitcase just then. When my face was passable, I took my cell phone from the pocket of my dress.

"It's as good a time as any..." I muttered to myself, preparing to destroy it. I almost had the battery slot open when it started vibrating in my hand. Dad was calling. His timing was either perfect or terrible, since in another few seconds he would have been sent to the eternal black hole that my voicemail inbox was about to become. I pressed the green button and lifted the phone to my ear.

"Hello?" I asked, as though I hadn't seen who was calling.

"Hey Ally, it's Dad. I just wanted to tell you that Mom's doctors said she can be discharged tomorrow. Isn't that great?" His voice wavered betraying his false optimism and revealing the exhaustion just under the surface.

"Yup, it's great." I glanced around the bathroom, white and mint green tile, as I waited for him to elaborate.

"Yeah. So... I'm sure she'd like to see you if you want to come over to the house in the next few days."

Ha. I doubted that. Even if she didn't know her pills had been switched, let alone that I did it, I knew she had her suspicions about my connection to Bruce's disappearance. My presence would probably cause another suicide attempt immediately if she was as unstable as she sounded.

"Actually, I'm not gonna be here," I told my dad. He grumbled in disgruntled confusion. "Robin and I are going on a trip."

"That doesn't make any sense, Allegra. What trip? Why would you go on vacation when your mother is in the hospital?"

"Well..." I grasped for a reason he might understand. "She got the tickets last-minute from a friend, and the dates were already set."

"Where are you going? When will you be back?"

I didn't want to answer truthfully and couldn't think of a lie that fast, so I decided it was time to end the conversation. "Oh shoot, Dad, they're calling our flight number. I'll text you when we get there!"

I almost hung up, but before I could push the button, he called me back with a, "Wait!"

I put the phone back to my ear. "Yeah?"

"Allegra…" The pause on the other end was so long that I thought we'd lost connection until I heard him inhale again. "Do you remember that one time when we came home and Mom was going nuts trying to chase down a fly?

"Yeah. Why?"

"Well, it may not have been there at all. Or maybe it was, and she overreacted. Your mom has been living with bipolar disorder, bipolar I, for longer than I've known her. She's been able to keep it controlled for years with meds and therapy. Actually, that fly thing was the last time I saw her out of control in any way."

"Dad, why are you telling me this?"

He sighed deeply. "I don't really know. We thought it was the best thing to keep her condition away from you kids. Didn't want you to have to live under the stigma of having a mentally ill mother. Maybe that wasn't the right thing to do. I just…"

"Well," I said, leaning against the cold sink and trying to keep my tone sympathetic. "It is kind of a surprise, but I guess it makes sense." Of course, it hadn't been a surprise since I had found her prescription bottle, but I couldn't tell him that.

"I'm sorry, Allegra. I don't mean to dump all this on you. We just haven't talked much since this whole thing started and I thought you should know."

"Oh… Okay. Thanks."

"I'm not sure if you even want to know all of this," he continued. "She didn't say I could tell you, but can't imagine she'd object to her own daughter knowing about her condition. Just wanted to keep you updated is all."

A mother and daughter in floor-length skirts and headscarves entered the bathroom, glanced at me the way most people glance at strangers in potentially shady public places, and made their way to two adjacent stalls.

I lowered my voice a little. "Has Mom said anything about why she… snapped? Maybe that's not the right word."

He let out a joyless chuckle. "No, no, it's as right as anything else. She hasn't said much about anything that's been bothering her since before Easter. I didn't even know she'd stopped taking her meds!" There was another pause, shorter this time. One of the toilets in the stalls behind me flushed. "Maybe she really did just snap. Maybe everyone eventually snaps."

I waited a few seconds to be respectful of my dad's existential crisis, then told him again that our flight was being called and that I had to go. I figured I'd be harder to find if he told the police, who would inevitably question him about my disappearance in connection with Nova's murder, that Robin and I were traveling together by plane. He told me to have a safe flight, seeming not to care anymore that he didn't know the destination. After we hung up, I removed the phone's SIM card and snapped it in half, wrapped it in a wet paper towel to destroy any life it might have left, and stuffed it deep into the trash bin. I dropped the remaining technological husk into my purse in case I needed it later, left the bathroom, and looked for a place to sit in the sleepy, run-down terminal.

Less than half the chairs were filled, so it was easy to find a spot that felt sufficiently isolated. Every once in a while, I felt eyes on me, which was to be expected since I was dressed for a nightclub but was sitting in a metal chair attached to the wall of a bus terminal. I didn't do anything while I waited, just sat still with my arms crossed and glanced surreptitiously at the other people waiting for rides when they were too busy to notice. The mother and daughter had returned from the bathroom and now poured over a crossword book together, pencils in hand. A nervous-looking teenage couple on one of the benches whispered with their heads together, looking exactly like they were Romeo-and-Julieting their way out of Arizona without their parents' knowledge. A scruffy guy with an oversized backpack sat on the floor in the corner, legs stretched out in front of him as he dozed. A couple rows away and facing me, a twenty-something guy in jeans, a t-shirt, and glasses read a book. He had glanced at me over the pages more than once and I'd politely pretended not to notice, but now I wondered if he could be part of my new plan.

I glanced around the room until I saw through the front window that the pay phone was right outside the door. Lugging my suitcase along, I limped outside and examined the setup. This was the first time in my life I was using a pay phone. Luckily for me and my suitcase, the phone wasn't inside an actual booth where Clark Kent might make a quick change into Superman, just three sides of clear plexiglass attached to the outside of the building that the caller could stand between. I dropped a few coins in the slot and dialed Robin's cell phone number from memory.

I expected the phone to ring until the very last second, when she would decide that she forgave me, pick up the phone, and find out where she could meet me. She would definitely have decided by now that she still wanted to be with me. How could she not, after all we'd done together? Also, how could she not, knowing I could expose her hit-and-run guilt at any time? For that matter, I had a feeling that my testimony of Robin actually delivering the fatal blow to Bruce by slashing his neck when I wasn't even in the room would definitely hold up in court. But it wouldn't come to that, of course. She was about to pick up the phone.

Four rings. Five. Six. Click. *We're sorry, the party you have reached...*

I hung up and fed more quarters into the machine. Maybe she hadn't heard the phone ring. Maybe she was in the shower or something. I dialed again. Six rings. Click. *We're sorry, the party you have reached...*

Two more quarters. One ring. Two rings. Three ri— *We're sorry...*

I slammed the phone back into its cradle and a few coins clattered into the return shoot. That fucking bitch. It was common knowledge that a lot of ringing before going to voicemail means the person you were trying to call hadn't touched the phone and probably wasn't near it. Going straight to voicemail meant the phone was off or dead. But if you only heard a few rings before it prompted you to leave a message— especially if it cut off in the middle of a ring—that almost certainly meant the person saw your call and hit the "ignore" button, actively sending you to their voicemail. She wasn't showering or asleep or listening to music too loudly to hear the phone ring. She knew this unknown number was me. She was ignoring me. She didn't care where I was going because she wasn't planning to join me.

She really was finished.

Well, that was fine. It would have been nice to start over with someone who already loved me, but whatever. I could do it alone, and probably better than if she was following behind me, always wringing her hands with worry that we might get caught. It was time to switch gears. I was officially doing this alone.

I took the foundation compact from my purse and used my fingertips to streak my eye makeup, checking the tiny mirror to make sure it looked believable. I pinched the sensitive underside of my arm as hard as I could until my eyes watered and I couldn't stand the pain anymore, and blinked to make sure the tears fell all the way down my cheeks. Then I did it again on the other arm, and even more moisture leaked from my eyes. Black streaked down my cheeks in a very noticeable way. I grabbed a few random handfuls of hair close to my scalp until it looked disheveled. The real limping I was doing as a result of walking several miles in heels could only help. I headed back inside, dragging my suitcase behind me as pathetically as I could.

The seat I'd been in earlier had not been occupied, so I flopped back into it, let out a huge sigh, and started rummaging frantically through my purse.

"Are you okay?" The guy with glasses asked, setting his book on the seat next to him.

I looked up at him and sniffed. His expression changed from curiosity to deep concern.

"I'm fine," I told him. "Just thought I had more money in here. Can't seem to find it."

"Well, did you want to get something from the vending machine or something? It can be my treat." He pulled a few dollars out of his pocket and showed them to me. "My name's Con."

I snorted. "Like 'con artist'?"

He smiled like he'd heard that one before. "No, like Constantine."

"Do your parents hate you?"

"Nah, they're just Greek." He chuckled and held up his cash again. "So, did you want something? I'm getting hungry myself, and my bus isn't supposed to be here for another half hour or so."

"No, I'm not hungry… I just thought I had more money. I…" I gave another exasperated sigh and sat back heavily against the metal chair. "I don't really know where I'm gonna end up so I at least wanted to have some money when I got there."

Con put the money back in his pocket and ran a hand through his dark, curly hair. "What do you mean you don't know where you're gonna end up?"

I knew that would catch his attention. Now it was time to seal the deal. I sniffed and rubbed my eye, further smearing the eyeliner that was already beyond repair. "Well, I was at a party with my boyfriend tonight, and when we got home, he just got really mean and told me he was kicking me out…" I paused and pretended to try not to cry, looking up at the ceiling to contain my fake tears.

Con moved seats so he was sitting next to me, but didn't touch me. "That's awful. Did he say why?"

I sniffed. "He saw me talking to some other guy and got jealous. I was just asking where the bathroom was!"

"Holy shit," he said thoughtfully, scratching the back of one hand with the nails of the other. He was a fidgeter. "That's awful, I'm so sorry… I didn't get your name."

That's because I didn't give it to you, I thought callously. "I'm Nova." It was the first name that came to mind besides my own, which I didn't think I should use if I was trying to fade into invisibility.

"Well, Nova, your story is terribly sad, but it does explain why you're the only one here dressed like you didn't just roll out of bed. Myself included."

"Yeah," I nodded down at my clothes, "He didn't let me change, just threw my stuff in a suitcase and told me to get out of there."

"What an asshole." Con shook his head.

"You said your bus leaves in half an hour… Are you going to Portland?"

"Yup. Going home from meeting up with some college friends for a reunion down here. I hadn't seen some of 'em in five years."

"Wow. How many people?"

"It ended up just being four of us, but it was epic!" He grinned with excitement.

"I'm going to Portland too. It was the only place on the list of tonight's departures that I've never been before."

He noticeably brightened when he heard we shared the same destination. "You know what?" he asked without waiting for a reply. "I saw one of those hot drink dispensers next to the vending machines. I'm gonna go get us a couple coffees, and we can talk shit on your ex-boyfriend until the bus comes." He stood up and started walking toward the hallway where bathrooms, drinking fountains, and vending machines were located.

I nodded, but then remembered the strong aroma of coffee in the apartment as I had finished packing earlier and scrunched up my nose with displeasure. "Maybe not a coffee. It's not really my thing. I bet the machine has hot chocolate, though?"

He snapped with both hands, then shot me double finger guns. "I bet it does," he said. "I'll be right back."

After Con got back with two steaming Styrofoam cups, we settled into small talk. I learned without any prompting that he actually lived a couple of hours south of Portland but enjoyed taking the train for the last leg of the journey. I learned that he was twenty-five years old, had a younger sister in high school, and parents who ran a small Greek restaurant together. I learned he lived alone but his family lived in Portland itself, so he might stop to visit before getting on the train home. I learned that he was the first person in his family to be born in America, the first to go to college, and the first not to speak a single word of the Greek language.

"Even my sister is trying to learn," he told me with laughter in his voice. "I just can't wrap my mind around all the..." He contorted his mouth and made a sound like a disgruntled whale. "Ya know...vowel sounds."

I laughed and punched him playfully on the arm. "Whatever that just was, it wasn't vowel sounds." He lightly shoved me back, grinning again.

Now that physical contact had been initiated, Con got very cozy very quickly. When it was time to get on the bus, he lifted my heavy suitcase into the luggage compartment underneath, then helped himself to the seat next to mine when I sat down. Within the first hour of the journey, he had his arm around my shoulders. I just let it happen because toward the end of the trip when he asked me to stay at his place for a while, it would have to be his idea. Otherwise, he'd always have a niggling thought at the back of his head that maybe I didn't really love him, maybe I was just using him for his resources until I could dispose of him and move on. The thing is, he would be right. He just couldn't begin to fathom the method of disposal.

EPILOGUE

Elena

August 2008

Today is my daughter's nineteenth birthday, and we haven't spoken to her since she disappeared two months ago. My husband, Michael, says it must just be a coincidence that she vanished the same night they found that poor girl dead in the high school theater. My son, Toby, says there's no such thing as coincidences, at least not in any murder movie he's ever seen, but he still doesn't think his sister could murder anyone, so someone must be framing her or something. I'm inclined to half-agree with Toby—there's no such thing as coincidences.

I had my first panic attack when I was in tenth grade, the same year bipolar disorder was inducted into the third edition of the Diagnostic and Statistical Manual of Mental Disorders. Psychiatric specialists told me I had an unspecified "mood disorder". That the faces I'd been seeing in wood grain and carpet vacuum lines my whole life weren't really there. That they'd be starting me on a drug called Lithium.

My diagnosis was officially amended to bipolar disorder shortly after graduating college. Since I now had a more specific diagnosis, I was able to get more personalized care than the one-size-fits-all "mood disorder" description and one-drug-cures-all Lithium prescription infamously doled out by so many doctors in the '80s. I tried a handful of different medications, some of which came with brutal side effects, and finally figured out a daily cocktail that kept me awake but not manic, calm but not depressed, and even sort of mitigated the fight or flight response artificially produced by panic attacks.

I had been dating Michael, a gawky wallflower with acne scars whose parents wanted him to become a pharmacist, for almost two years. Just like everything else life threw at him, he took my diagnosis in stride. He had already accepted the things my mental illness made me do and say as parts of me—and, therefore, parts of our relationship. He wasn't too bothered when I screamed with night terrors at two a.m. or threw a whole rotisserie chicken in the garbage before returning the empty plastic case to its spot in the fridge. He perfected the art of comforting, not confronting. He actually understood, as much as a mentally well person can, how much the illness affected my everyday life and how hard I worked to maintain equilibrium.

Michael and I graduated at the same time, me with a BA in English and him with a BS in Chemistry. He had absolutely no intention of using this degree to continue in pharmaceutical studies, so shortly before we moved in together, he took a night job moving freight around a warehouse and decided to "figure the rest out later."

I was accepted into a master's program for social work the following year, which felt insanely productive for someone who routinely spent thirty-six hours in bed when she was depressed. While Michael slept during the day after his strenuous graveyard shifts, I was a busy graduate student and intern on the inpatient psychiatric treatment floor of a hospital. Outside of school, I went to all my appointments, took my meds on time, and dutifully reported any changes to my psychiatrist. I learned to be a model mental health patient because I hated how I felt when I wasn't.

I became pregnant with Allegra in my final semester of grad school, so Michael and I hurried to the courthouse for a quickie wedding between midterms. We decided he would continue working nights so we could live the new American dream of being a two-income household that also doesn't have to pay for childcare. A lot of young couples find their lives falling apart with the introduction of an unexpected baby, but we felt strangely ready for her arrival.

Unfortunately, I was so busy worrying about all the regular pregnancy roadblocks like constantly having to pee, shifting organs, stretch marks, hemorrhoids, heartburn, and incessant nausea, I didn't even consider what changes I might need to make to my medication. My doctor recommended a short weaning period of six weeks, after which I wouldn't take anything but prenatal vitamins until she was born.

Every second of that pregnancy was ten times worse than any side effect Michael had ever seen me experience. He did what he could—got me the foods I was craving and rubbed my swollen feet—but he couldn't stop what was happening in my head. My unbalanced brain was marinating, unprotected by the scientific barrier it had become used to over the last decade, in a soup of pregnancy hormones. The design on the wooden slats in the floor of our apartment's balcony turned from simple knots and lines into ghostly faces howling to be let out. Kitchen knives glinted happily at me from the drying rack, inviting me to slice open my arms and rip out my veins as I emptied the dishwasher. *No, wait,* they sometimes told me, *we were mistaken. Don't cut yourself, Elena. Cut out the parasite they all say is a baby.* I went into labor in the middle of the night. Michael said he didn't even realize I was out of bed until he got up to use the bathroom and found me perched on the edge of the couch, silently using all eight fingers to claw strips of skin off of my own thighs. I didn't remember getting up.

I was too far along for an epidural by the time we arrived at the hospital. The pain, bright lights, lack of medication, and countless people in scrubs sticking their faces and hands in my cervix were too much to bear. I tried to bite, scratch, and spit at most of the nursing staff whenever they tried to help me through a contraction. They couldn't hand me the baby when she was out because my wrists and ankles had been bound to the bed with flexible blue straps. They handed her to Michael and immediately flooded my IV with a sedative.

During the generously long (albeit unpaid) paternity leave Michael received from the warehouse, I managed to finish my internship, graduate, and find my full-time job with Foundation House. I was also back on my regular cocktail of bipolar meds, but they teamed up with the leftover pregnancy hormones to make me a screaming, sobbing mess daily. Before bringing Allegra home from the hospital, Michael and I joked that I had the easier childcare duties since he'd be with her during the day and I would take nights. I knew I'd be getting up for feedings every few hours, but I never could have predicted that the first year of Allegra's life would be even worse than the experience of bringing her into the world.

Once we began our new daily routine, I stopped sleeping. Allegra cried nonstop when nothing appeared to be wrong. I'd rock her for hours, finally getting her little eyes to flutter shut, and set her in the crib with no problem, but as soon as I sat on the living room couch or tried to lie down for five minutes in my bed, the wailing began again. I know a baby couldn't possibly time something like that, but it was like she knew I was finally getting a second to decompress and wouldn't allow it. This went on all night, every night, for over a year. I thought it was just my body being mean to me, that sleep deprivation was teaming up with postpartum hormones and my mood stabilizers to make taking care of a fussy baby feel worse than it actually was. *All new mothers deal with this*, I assured myself time and time again as I sponged spit-up off my shirt and prepared to coast through another work day on nothing but caffeine and crossed fingers.

I tried to keep up with all the new symptoms so I could report them to my doctor, but it was hard to know exactly where reality stopped. I heard babies crying through the walls of my cubicle at work or coming through the car radio speakers during my commute. When I was home with the baby at night there were figures lurking outside her bedroom windows or in the darker corners of the house. They usually turned out to be a coat thrown over a chair or street lights casting a weird shadow, but rationality didn't stop me from being terrified. On the rare occasions that Allegra slept for more than a few minutes, Michael found me crouching in the entryway clutching a closed umbrella as a weapon in case the figures were real.

Allegra started keeping secrets when she was three. They began as things that would only be important to a preschooler, like not wanting to get in trouble for putting the empty bag back into the pantry after eating the last cookie. She stopped showing me the pictures she colored, opting to hide them in her closet or just tear them into pieces. When I snuck into her closet and looked at the pictures while she slept, I understood why. In a child's messy crayon scrawl, approximations of humans gaped with eyes and mouths rounded in surprise, knives sticking out of their stomachs or necks or legs. The faces looked eerily similar to the ghosts screaming in the balcony wood slats.

Terms like *antisocial personality disorder* and *callous and unemotional traits* flashed through my brain, remnants from grad school textbooks, but I dismissed them as quickly as they appeared. I assumed she had caught bits and pieces of violent TV shows—even though we did our best to keep those away from her—and this was her way of processing what she saw. I reminded myself not to diagnose everyone, especially not my toddler, based on a single piece of evidence. I left the pictures where they were and backed quietly out of the dark room.

Getting pregnant with Toby was a welcome accident when Allegra was five. By this time, I had a different OBGYN and a different psychiatrist, both of whom agreed on bipolar meds I could take while pregnant that wouldn't harm either of us. Because of this, the pregnancy was such a dream that I sometimes forgot I was pregnant at all until a stranger asked how far along I was or tried to touch my belly. During that pregnancy, we moved from the apartment to our little house in Mesa. Michael was let go from the warehouse and found his overnight job at the bakery, which was great because instead of coming home in the mornings smelling like sweat and forklift chain lubrication oil, he brought the delightful scents of dough and powdered sugar.

Allegra was sometimes nearby when I dropped my pills for the week into the little plastic container with a slot for each day.

"This one is to keep Mommy happy and energetic so she can play with you," I would say about my mood stabilizer as the pill thunked into the bottom of the container.

"Can I try?" she would ask.

"Sure, you do the next one. This is a vitamin to make my bones and muscles strong while I grow your baby brother. It also helps him grow big and strong enough to come out and be a kid like you!" I would hand her the round, chalky prenatal vitamins, looking larger in her hand than they did in mine, and she would drop one into each slot.

Since discovering her drawings, it had become a habit to check her "secret" hiding place after she fell asleep at night. A week or two after she first helped me with my pills, I found my bottle of prenatal vitamins buried deep under a pile of blankets and stuffed animals in her closet. I thought she probably just wanted to grow strong too, and her kindergartener brain told her these vitamins would do the trick. I was thankful that the child-proof cap had prevented her from opening it and eating too many.

I would hardly allow myself to consider the possibility that she didn't want the vitamins at all—she just didn't want me to have them. It was totally irrational, I told myself after this thought flashed through my mind, to think a child that young would wish harm on her mother and unborn brother to the point that she would steal what makes the baby "grow big and strong." I didn't think her brain was even capable of making those connections yet, but now I'm not so sure.

•➤

I told Michael I don't remember much about the day I was trying to chase down the fly and ended up trashing the living room. He mentioned it when I was in the hospital recently, so he must remember it pretty often too.

While he was at work the night before, Allegra had a more difficult night than usual. Even though she had finally started to sleep through the night while I was pregnant with Toby, his arrival had triggered her nighttime behavior to regress. She started vehemently competing with her newborn brother for my attention.

She heard me puttering around the house in the middle of the night, feeding and changing the baby with the TV on in the background, and started hollering that I needed to come in there right now. She wanted a glass of water. She wanted another bedtime story. She wanted to know where we go when we die, what happened to the dinosaurs, and where babies come from. The fifth time I entered her room that night, I tried to explain why it would be the last time until morning.

"Sweetheart," I said, trying to mask my exasperation. "This is just how babies are. They need a lot of attention. You're a big kid who can feed yourself and go to the bathroom on your own. Toby can't do any of that for himself, so he needs me to do it for him. You were the same way when you were his age."

"Then why does he get to be awake all night and not me?" she yelled, her little face scrunched up with indignation.

"Well, because you do all your eating and pooping during daylight hours. Babies aren't so lucky—they do it around the clock."

Allegra refused to accept this. She screamed at me that I must not be a very good mommy if I can't take care of both my kids at the same time. Her fury ramped up into a tantrum before I could even think about how to stop it. I left her in her room, throwing her possessions to the ground as she cried and shrieked unintelligible words that were probably more attacks on my parenting. When I checked back twenty minutes later, her rage had lulled her to sleep, little blonde head resting peacefully on a pile of destroyed picture books.

The next day, Saturday, Michael offered to take Allegra out of the house for a while so Toby and I could have some quiet feeding and play time. Before they left, I asked Allegra to help me get the baby dressed. She huffed and rolled her eyes like she was sixteen, not six, before following me into Toby's room. The baby was squirmy and uncooperative as usual, wailing loudly no matter how I tried to comfort him, and it was Allegra's job to help me hold his delicate limbs in place as I covered them with clothing. She stood on a chair so she could reach him on the changing table. At one point, he spat up all over the table and every article of clothing I had brought over. I went back to the dresser to find more, tasking Allegra with making sure her brother didn't fall on the floor. She had both hands on him when I turned my back, diligently doing her job. Toby's cries continued unabated until I turned back and distractedly stuffed him into a onesie and some tiny cotton pants.

We finished getting him dressed, and Allegra left with her dad. Toby fell asleep as soon as the car left the driveway, and woke up a couple hours later needing to be changed. I unbuttoned his onesie and was surprised to find several red welts on his belly that hadn't been there earlier. One even had the dark sheen of a bruise starting to form along the edge. It looked almost like someone had pinched him, but pinching that hard, not to mention more than once, wouldn't be an accident. I knew immediately that Allegra must have done this when I'd been looking for more clothes, but I didn't even allow the thought to keep forming before I pushed it away. How could I accuse one of my children of hurting the other?

Before I could consider it anymore, something tiny and black zoomed through my peripheral vision. Between sleep deprivation and the lack of total certainty that I had taken my meds that morning, I wasn't sure it was real until I saw it land on the light blue wall. It was a large horsefly, the kind with little jaws shaped like scissors to cut through human skin so they could easily drink the blood. They were an annoyance to adults, but potentially dangerous to babies, so I began the chase. By the time I managed to get it out of Toby's room, the baby had fallen asleep again, so I closed the door and let him rest.

The fly may have slipped back outside when Michael and Allegra opened the front door. Maybe it was sucked into the AC unit and eviscerated. Maybe it really was still buzzing around the house, taunting me into a search. Maybe it was never there.

I didn't notice right away that they were back. The situation they walked into must have made me look completely unhinged. I saw the little black flash again, then unmistakably, a fat black fly perched on Allegra's hair clip. I approached her with the fly swatter and had almost decided on the angle of my smack before I noticed the apprehension in her face. For a few scary seconds, before reasoning caught up with impulse, I had been ready to hit her. Then the fly either buzzed away or disappeared, and I chased it into the kitchen.

Later that afternoon, I asked Michael not to talk about my mental illness with Allegra anymore. I told him I was going to stop having her help me sort my pills, and it would be better if she didn't even know anything was wrong with me. Toby too, when the time came. Michael was resistant to the idea at first, but he had to agree with me that kids don't need to be overburdened with their parents' issues. This was a good argument that got him on my side, and it wasn't necessarily a lie, but it also wasn't the whole truth. I didn't want Allegra to see my weaknesses anymore, especially if I had to start keeping her away from her brother. I didn't tell

Michael about my suspicion that she had hurt Toby, didn't even tell him about the welts, but I kept them in the back of my mind and didn't leave her alone with him again until he was old enough to defend himself.

Being hospitalized for a suicide attempt was a surreal experience. It was the first time I've ever had to go inpatient. I don't remember driving away from work in the middle of the day, nor do I remember swerving so intentionally into the concrete freeway median. I don't remember them checking my ID in the emergency room, pulling my digital chart, and noticing that I should be on a pretty serious dose of psych meds absent from my bloodwork. I do, however, remember them accusing me of intentionally not taking my pills. I emphatically insisted through the haze of a mild concussion that I had been taking them, I always took them, just ask my psychiatrist. I also remember them asking if the crash had been an attempt to end my life, and taking my silence as a yes.

It wasn't necessarily an attempt to kill myself. Logically, I know that I have a lot to live for. I genuinely love my job, my husband, my life. I had just been feeling so bad, so off, for so many weeks that I didn't know what else to do but die. The unexplained shift to brain fog, depression, and increased panic attacks after so many successful years on the same medication convinced me that they hadn't stopped working, I had just become untreatable. If they couldn't help me anymore, there was no alternative but to cease existing altogether.

I understand why the doctors, and even Michael, didn't believe me. Blood tests don't lie, and people often do. I had no explanation for the complete lack of Seroquel in my system, and psych patients often stretch the truth about how good they are at remembering to take their meds. Even after appealing to Michael that he knows how consistent I've always been, he insisted that I must have just been forgetting to take that one when I grabbed the others. He didn't even check the almost-empty prescription bottle that would have contradicted his suspicion.

In addition to confusion about why my pills had suddenly stopped working, I was distraught about Bruce's disappearance. It had been more than three months since he'd checked in at Foundation House, and his handful of friends hadn't heard from him. This wouldn't normally have been totally out of character for a transient kid like Bruce, but he and I had an agreement. He liked to brag about how easy it was to skip town without a trace, so I asked him to let me know if he was ever going to leave Arizona. He hadn't wanted to, but after some convincing, he agreed, and I believed him. He was unreliable and a bit of a smart ass, but there was a really sweet kid underneath all those protective layers.

The week after Allegra visited, Foundation House held a beading workshop. I had a light workload that day, so I decided to participate in the class. I sat with Bruce and a couple other boys his age because they were the most vocally unenthused by the activity. As our group went through the tin of plastic beads provided by the instructor, I commented on the swirl and dot patterns etched into each one. Bruce and I organized patterns of beads based on their etchings, then by size, and finally by color. He decided to use only red beads and a simple ABAB pattern of swirls, dots, swirls, dots. When the bracelet was finished, he was the only boy at the table who didn't think wearing his creation was uncool. He slipped it onto his wrist with a broad grin and then sauntered off to find a snack.

Maybe the bracelet Allegra wore on Toby's birthday wasn't the same one. Maybe, like the fly, like the faces in wood grain, my vision was distorted by my broken brain. Maybe Allegra had had a fit of creativity one day and bought a pack of the same beads to make herself a bracelet. An identical bracelet, all in red, with the exact same design pattern. I know Michael thought I was nuts when I brought it up, because it really does seem like a crazy last resort to accuse your own child of someone else's disappearance when there are so many easier explanations. I let it drop that day in the kitchen, but I didn't stop thinking about it.

Weeks later, Bruce was still missing and Allegra didn't wear the bracelet in front of me again. That, in itself, was suspicious. I spent that time trying to figure out if they had a connection, but my detective skills are extremely limited, and my ability to concentrate started going fuzzy some time after Easter. This felt like a coincidence at the time, but now that I'm back to my regular routine, I'm seeing the whole situation more clearly.

If there's no such thing as coincidences, here's what I think happened. I think Bruce and Allegra must have made some kind of connection the day she visited Foundation House. They probably exchanged phone numbers and met up at some point after the bead workshop. Then he either gave her the bracelet, or she took it. When she realized that I recognized it, she tampered with my pills in hopes that would distract me from wondering why she had something that belonged to him. I have no idea how easy or difficult it might be to find placebos that look exactly like certain pills, but if she can make a seventeen-year-old disappear without a trace, I'm sure she could do something like that.

I can't bring myself to speculate any further, because I'm afraid I'm right. I should have shown Michael the violent drawings. I should have told him about her pinching baby Toby. I should have done more than just supervise their interactions looking for more red flags. I should have more vehemently insisted we find a child psychologist when she showed no interest in having friends, participating in extracurriculars, or decorating her bedroom as a pre-teen, or in high school when she seemed to choose the dance team at random to placate me instead of out of any actual interest. Without any of the background information that I'd been hiding for eighteen years, it's no wonder he dismissed my concerns as the ramblings of a crazy woman when I tried to tell him about the bracelet. I spent my life denying what my daughter is, worked as hard on that as I have on regulating my own mental state, and now it's too late to pull back the curtain and show everything I've hidden.

I can't help but wonder whether Allegra has ever appreciated, or even been aware, that I've been strategically ignoring some of her behavior in the interest of sheltering my child. The only reason she's been able to operate under this flawless, manipulative, vindictive persona all these years is because I've allowed it. I saw it unfolding and insisted there was nothing wrong. I didn't want her to be like me, dependent on a handful of pills for the rest of her life because of the way she sees the world. I should have said something when I was still credible enough to be listened to, even by my own husband. Now I don't know where she is, and I can't protect her anymore.

About the Author

Jes Pan (they/them) wrote their first book at age two, providing illustrations and dictating the words for "Lolo Zookeeper, Hiding Crocodile." They went on to publish hundreds of home-printed masterpieces at Lolo Press, the pretend publishing company inspired by their childhood nickname.

Jes's love of stories and books grew as they got older, and they continued to read and write voraciously into adulthood. One BA in Creative Writing, one Master's in Library Science, four years working retail, and five years as a librarian later, Jes is finally revisiting their original love of words and the way they fit together. They edited The Legacy He Left Me by Lovern Gordon in 2021, a life-changing foray into the world of professional publishing. Sonder is their first novel.

Jes lives in Arizona with their wife and two tiny dogs. They are active in the LGBTQ+ community, mainly facilitating informal education programs for youth and young adults through the public library and non-profit organizations. They also love to knit, craft, read, make spreadsheets, connect on TikTok, and consume horror content of (almost) any kind.

9 7 9 8 8 8 5 8 9 1 9 2 9